Voices Unheard, Words Unspoken

By Jim Oshust

"Patriotism is supporting your country all the time and the government when it deserves it"

Samuel L. Clemmons (Mark Twain)

Dedication

To those at the back of the crowd who are never heard,

And so often unseen

Contents

Before the reader proceeds, allow me to state unequivocally that the following contains the data gathered, repetition of facts provided by supposedly valid sources and personal opinions of an American citizen who would be considered at an advanced age. The writer professes no accelerated acumen that would provide him an academic status or political perspicacity greater than others. I am not an attorney nor have I ever been to law school. Because of the nature of my career in management of entertainment, sports and exposition facilities and dealing with hundreds of contracts for featured events at these facilities plus a number of major sports events, I became very interested in the rights of the patron. Basically the ticket buyer, the event participants and employees of those facilities. This led to desiring a thorough understanding of the U.S. Constitution that encompasses such rights. Although not really a list of laws, the constitution rather presents the caveats regarding both permissions and prohibitions relative to the treatment of the citizen as affected by the judicial, law enforcement and regulatory agencies of local, state and national government.

The ideological or cultural bent of this book will tend to be traditionally conservative as concerns appreciation of my country, desire to see the rule of law pursued and the acceptance of my fellow man's right to receive equal treatment in all matters and the belief in the value of life. Still, I am more liberal in the need to provide security for all persons and institutions and respect for those freedoms equated in the U.S. Constitution. I care for our domestic pets and the magnificent members of our wild kingdom. I have an intense interest in the welfare of the impoverished, the physically and mentally incapacitated, our children and those of the religious inclination with whom I may not agree, but will always support their right to follow the doctrine or faith of their choosing. That being said, let us begin.

To be succinct and on point. I dislike governmental types who reconfigure their moral, ethical and original personas to feed their own demand for continuing power. Who disregard or inattentive to adherence and dedication to those by whom they were elected and are responsible to serve. They are the virus or disease more deadly than any we suffer today. I am concerned about the influence those with academic, cultural and celebrity status have on the lesser aware of many sensitive and troubling issues we face. They are the strident and often shrill voice of ideologies yet to be fully explained and even more suspiciously supported, either by legal position or undisclosed funding.

We are being ruled by mediocrity. We are being infected by a virulent strain of imposed self-importance by a leadership who have no more right to control our personal destinies than the US Constitution allows. Our principal executive and legislative figures are assuming a dominance that is an antithesis to the basic freedoms guaranteed us in the original founding documents. Freedoms guaranteed by the blood and sacrifice of thousands of Americans throughout our two hundred and fifty year existence. There, you have the collective reasoning for any of my commentary found within this manuscript.

Chapter 1

Prelude to the a Presidency

At 12:12 noon, Wednesday, January 20, 2021, Joseph Robinette Biden was inaugurated, during a brevity designed ceremony, as the 46th President of the United States. Just a few minutes prior, Kamala Darvi Harris was sworn in as Vice President of the United States, becoming the first female, or one of color to ever hold that position and at the highest level ever ever attained by a woman in our national government. The reduced spectacle, so part of this quadrennial occasion was limited by both a devastating pandemic entitled as Covid-19 virus, coupled with potential threats of violence stemming from a serious and riotous assault on the Capitol building on Jan. 6. A dangerously violent attempt to access the congressional chambers where voting on acceptance of the prior Electoral College ballots submitted was in process.

It was apparent we had just emerged from a season of dissent and entering a period of national discontent and potential social disorder. On Tuesday, November 3, 2020, the election of Joseph Biden as President of the United States was the result of collecting sufficient Electoral College and popular votes to replace the then incumbent chief executive, Donald J. Trump. Along with the swearing in of Biden, the installation of Harris as Vice President, until that time, the Junior Senator from California. Biden himself had served as Vice President in the Barack Obama administration for eight years, prior to that tenure, was for thirty-six years a U.S. Senator from Delaware, having spent the prior three as a local county council member and one year as a public defender. A total of 48 years supping at the public trough. Mathematically he would be the oldest President of the United State, being seventy-eight when he was inaugurated on January 20, 2021.

Kamala Harris had previously also been the Attorney General of California and prior to that, District Attorney for San Francisco. Another elevated political figure having dined at the tax supported buffet for the previous seventeen years. Whomever may not have any substantively detailed knowledge of either individual, I leave all the additional genealogy references and background data and rumor to those who normally babble on incessantly about such matters already widely publicized and of little interest to many. One fact remains clear and undeniable, unlike many other election campaign soirees, these two individuals were polar opposites, which may become quite clear as their administration proceeds. Her seemingly vindictive verbal assaults on Biden during the ill planned and ideologically amorphous Democratic debate series in 2020, may have cut into Biden's persona greatly. However, in the world of politics, bleeding from the arrows and semantic stabs of opponents quickly ceases when bureaucratic advantage raises its usual pustule head.

Unfortunately, during the entirety of the previous spring and through the fall, the American public was faced with a rampant promotion by certain groups to encourage detestation of all that was tradition, our nation's history and its present form of government. Violence became the mantra of protesting groups or at least the core contingent of agitators who seemed to be present at ever such demonstration. Possibly the riotous binges of destruction and injury was an exhibition of opposition to the incumbent president or was designed to produce a new vision encompassed in the more liberal and progressive approach to the myriad of social and economic global relationship issues facing the country at this time. That quandary I leave to the pompous pundits of political ideology. Regardless, the upcoming national election was touted as a split in the road, a new direction. Either a continuation on a road some declared was leading to economic and social disaster or a wider, more hopeful vision of a new and regenerated America. This was the choice voters faced in one of those most controversial elections in the history of our country.

The incumbent promised to continue on the path marked by the previous four years, promising to end the incessant and insidious lack of compromise of the elected Congress. To reduce what he contended was the stranglehold on the country's economic and social malaise by the legislative refusal to present and provide substantive resolution of what he claimed were the country's deficiencies created by past administrations. That campaign declaration was refuted by a majority of the voters, while interestingly enough, still leaving a minority margin of approximately seventy-four million, a figure far greater than any garnered by any winner or loser of prior elections. His opposition demanded a new direction resolving what they claimed had been four years of deterioration of social values and the economic future of the nation.

This book doesn't deal with the vagaries of either side of those disputes and policy controversies. Its intent is to present particular approaches as to the current delegation of credit and blame, depending on which side of the eventual result you reside which made it the most intense and conflictive campaign in the nation's electoral history. The stench of political rancor and violation of the most basic precepts of civility still haunts the chambers and hallways of Congress. It continues to divide this nation and is no longer mere campaign rhetoric but the reflection of personal animus toward each other and disregard for the people the political figures were elected to serve.

When this book was in its initial editing, only a few weeks remained before Election Day and I remembered the words of Prussian General, Carl von Clausewitz who wrote in his thesis, "On War, 1812; any plans that have no room for the unexpected can only lead to disaster." This comment was well tested in the strategy of both candidates as will be later mentioned several times. The 2020 election will have have become just a part of recent history before anyone ever actually reads this particular work. The public will be inundated by the wherewithal's and what if's of campaign tactics by both candidates as well as those factors and existing situations that may or may not have had any relevance to the final vote count. Regardless, the writer feels it important that at least one voice from the back of the crowd be heard. At least one observer of the then passing parade of political characterization, caprice and the calumny, be made available. To record a few impressions of this quadrennial event which became more a personal quest for power and domination than concern for the greater good of the citizenry and the nation as a whole.

So many books and essays, lengthy dissertations will in time present rather bizarre explanations and introspections of our government, too often merely decimated acres of forestland. Still, we will survive and in most cases prosper. British Jurist, Lord Scarma, 1911-2004, noted head of the English law Commission, stated, "A government above the law is a menace to be defeated". With such a direction, could that have caused the recent plethora of violent upheaval, accused insurrection and aggressive protest being the only means to achieve desired change? We leave that to the more enlightened in that field of curiosity.

Perhaps, when the 2020 national election's resulting commentary becomes inconsequential due to more pressing individual and public concerns, what is written herein will also join the chronicles of the forgotten or ignored. Yet, there must come a time when the thoughts and voices of the average citizen are ensconced in some archive. I have no unique knowledge of all such matters. I own no plethora of academic awards or publicly acclaimed insight into such specific issues. But, perhaps, at least it could be available in the still existing libraries, so some future inhabitant of this amazing land, has the opportunity to review what, along with the then voluminous commentary by others and existing media, would be what actually occurred. In reality, what were the facts as then happening? Which by any future date, all other accounts will have been massaged through the mishandling of those who would prefer to shelve into anonymity the unvarnished truth. Yet, the saying of Jorge `George' Santayana, Spanish philosopher and poet may remain the most cogent response to those who aren't concerned or would forget; "Those who cannot remember the past are condemned to repeat it."

Most certainly, the reticence of the loser of the 2020 election, Donald Trump, to refuse to concede when it became apparent he'd not mustered the sufficient votes to succeed himself, will fill a large portion of documentaries and media generated discussion. The endless onslaught of Donald Trump and his closest supporters to declare fraudulent or "fixed election result" claims, engendered a deluge of litigations in numerous state courts and became basic fodder for media concentration on the emergence of a new resident in the Oval Office. This writer believes firmly that, although there were myriads of ballot irregularities, brought on by mishandling, through incompetence or purposely altered to influence the other candidate and such charges, accusations, valid or not may never disappear, regardless, the final result legitimately favored the ultimate victor.

What is most concerning is the evidence of such numerous vote collection and calculation errors and miscues. Considering human beings were in charge of the entire vote validation process, the erroneous counting may well have existed as it has in the past – flawed human workers doing a tedious function in an ever required shorter time. But to what degree we may never definitively know. Did the curling smoke of corrupt electoral conduct, allegedly seen by some, may have proven the fact of contended irregularities? There were evident flaws in the system, locally and statewide.

Yet, I don't know and as supposedly rising from numerous election counting locations, do such claims and accusations really indicate the smoldering embers of corruption and illegal tactics? Or just the normal dissatisfaction with both the slowness of results and either loss or gain recorded for or against either candidate. In the opinion of many Trump supporters, there were overt acts by individual election workers or supervising staff to alter final returns. Again, their constitutional right to contest but little definitive proof they occurred.

It may soon be shown that three primary factors had a much greater impact on final counts than any inappropriate actions. In simple terms, incompetence in supervision of the process in many locations. The lack of sufficient training required to maintain the flow of ballot enumeration and validation and not least, the evident insufficiency of a poorly or little tested software programming to make the task less complicated. There remains a bone of contention regarding the allowance of a quickly revised process involving unwarranted and massive surge of mail-in ballots, the most in the history of any election. The multitude of complaints and avowed discovery of irregularities, whether factual, intended or accidental, have provided conspiracy apologists the shadowy specter of corruption that this writer feels will never be proven or disallowed in the minds of the loser's supporters.

What this cacophony of claimants did clearly reveal, the absolute and immediate need to closely review the entire election balloting process and method of verifying those same cast votes. This should be the responsibility of the incoming national and state administrations. It could become a true legacy of the Biden tenure and will be mentioned later.

Largely reported was the often stated intentions by a particular Democrat spokes persons that if Trump were to be reelected, the desire to energize removal of him would continue even after his vacating the Oval office. It became a constitutional question which may or may not need to become an item on the United States Supreme Court agenda. Still, there was initiated a second impeachment effort by the House of Representative's Democratic majority just a few weeks before Trump's departure from the presidency. The House effort was successful in the heat of Democratic confidence they would re regain the majority. It was later rebuked in the Senate vote, nonsensically after Trump once again became a private citizen. The principal charge that he'd incited vocally the tragic and disturbing January 6, 2021 attack by surging mobs on the capitol building where the earlier votes by the Electoral College were being counted and by certain opponents who argued they were not legitimate, and were being refuted.

That incident, garnering reams of misquoted, misconstrued and automatically biased presentation by the media, will be argued for years to come. As to the charge that Trump was directly responsible for urging and literally inciting the crowds that breached the Capitol Building is a subject I'd rather leave up to those whose preeminent hatred for him will give them the energy to continue their prosecution efforts.

Several weeks of the legislature's time was consumed in preparing, submitting and implementing the second impeachment and ultimate trial of Donald J. Trump. As the vote in the Senate required two thirds to convict, it was assumed far in advance that the entire episode was, in the opinion of several individuals well versed in such matters, merely political theater, common inside the "Beltway." Trump was not convicted, the targeted intent to deny him any future opportunity to run again for any federal office quashed. More important has to be recognition by many in the general public of the increase in pure hate emanating from those favoring assault on an Individual who was no longer within the domain of an elected federal official. To some it was a blatant attempt to continue pursuit of their dreaded nemesis which made for explosively challenging comments and hopefully emotion stirring TV talk. Sadly for the attackers it came to naught. Their next hope, a plethora of indictments, convictions, and to the ardent anti-Trump contingent, perhaps incarceration to be provided by state and federal law enforcement and judicial sources.

For the moment, a bit of review, the Democratic Party, victorious in attaining the White House this time, did interestingly lose their formerly larger majority in the House of Representatives and were forced to face an unassailable mathematical truth. Although Joseph Biden earned, at final count, possibly over eighty million votes, Donald Trump received in excess of seventy-four million votes. A measurable force of public involvement to say the least. To charge into the labyrinth of legal maneuvers to further denigrate and punish him for their contended misdeeds in and out of office could quickly alienate not only his support mass but challenge the more composed nature of many who voted for Biden more to see specific changes in the previous quadrennial of conflict and and inacceptable conduct on both sides of the aisle. A voting group who would be more likely to contend, the election is over, a new administration is moving in place. Why carry on this type of pointed revenge when what was desired was return to normalcy, earlier declared by their candidate, Joe Biden? Political reprisal is a two sided sword. A weapon, when flourished inaccurately and carelessly that can also endanger the user.

In keeping with his sweeping declaration of immediate and multiple changes in the former administrative actions, Biden then, on the first moment of his Oval office occupancy, embarked on what numerous observers felt was a most damaging approach to a new administration. He signed into issuance a myriad of Executive orders, numbering over fifty such dictates. Aside from those measures intended to deal with the Covid-19 crisis and ensuing pandemic, others were simply to stop any further action on programs, directives or legislative participation sponsored by the prior resident of the White House. This almost hysterically motivated surge of such orders were in total contrast to previous presidents. In those instances, a few days would be used to take up in consultation with the victorious leadership, purposeful delineation of what task or prominent national need should be dealt with first.

In completing this marathon of instantaneous change, his unannounced flurry of actions created questions. Was it retribution against his predecessor's prior control or merely fulfilling dictates from a shadow influence controlled by certain members of the Democratic Party leadership? An inquiry still to be answered but portending a possible misalignment between the Executive and legislative branches of government as stipulated in the Constitution. If it continues further into the Biden term, there is a danger of inferring a total control none of the three branches can claim.

Those who foster a single ideology in order to garner the greatest support must keep in mind the time not that far in the past when there was another candidate – a third party competitor. In 1992 election, Texas industrialist Ross Perot earned an impressive 19% of the total vote in his battle against the then Democratic candidate, Bill Clinton and his opponent, incumbent

Republican President, George H. W. Bush. Although not winning, Perot came back in 1995, again facing off against Bill Clinton, that time achieving a lower 8% of the vote. But numbers do count, particularly when the voting margins are expected to be much closer. A situation reminiscent of the quote by African American professional baseball notable, Satchel Paige when he reportedly quipped, "Don't look back. Something might be gaining on you."

In the mad rush to equate this victory as justified and necessary to remove the tarnish on our national image, vocally declared by both the Democratic Party and the media, forgotten by many but still a very evident truth, the results of the 2016 election. Regardless of the self-endowed political savants, Donald J. Trump was handed the 2016 Presidential win by a trio of unlikely colleagues. First, the totally mismanaged and lethargic candidacy of an individual who was provided access to a nomination that had never been contested. Hillary Rodham Clinton did gain the majority of popular votes which did little more than give her supporters a small claim to the unfairness of the Electoral College – a subject yet to be discussed herein.

Next, the savage and vitriolic condemnation of the Republican candidate by the media to a degree that their muchly vaunted positon of fairness was seriously damaged. A demonstration of pure bias and engineered omission and redirection of truth may never allow them to reclaim its once cherished image. Their unequivocal support of one candidate and equal printed and broadcasted abuse of the other, rallied an undercurrent of dissatisfaction with their conduct that moved many undecided to Trump's side. Embarrassingly it was the embedded Republican leadership, what became referred to as the "anti Trumpers", the very people who were to carry forth the banners promoting their nominee.

Amazed and disheartened that an outlander, an upstart had gained the nomination, they apparently determined to remain non-committal and too often silent as to participation in the ensuing campaign. So as to conserve their image and power base, they did little – if nothing. And with a combination of self-serving arrogance of Clinton herself and her campaign staff, coupled with a leash controlled media, allowed Trump a pseudo posture of being from the people. The blustery, often intemperate newcomer had however become the symbol of the general public's disgust with a current political and legislative system that fouled the airways with insincere rhetoric and the Halls of Congress with disillusionment. The lack of movement on recognized public issues, always the economy, maintenance of public good order, the various social ills that included racial imbalance, poverty, homelessness and the ever increasing access of undocumented individuals from the impoverished nations of Central America. The lethargy on the part of the elected representatives provide Trump and his supporters the needed impetus of which he took immediate advantage of and thus gained the necessary electoral votes.

If the continuing claim that a "deep state," exists, it would have to be a conglomeration of those not only opposed to a Trump like contender, but an innate desire to totally control any government, whomever resides at 1600 Pennsylvania Ave. This writer doesn't have any definitive knowledge of any such organized cabal. Yet, there was a concentrated and high organized and equally financed campaign against Trump's nomination and eventual election. One that continued posthaste throughout his entire term. If this is how all future election campaigns and ensuing executive tenures must endure, so be it. I have not the time left on this mortal domain or the wherewithal to change what may become the standard for either opposition against or media based support of any such adversarial adventures. We'll leave that subject to others better versed than I in such internal intrigue.

Chapter 2

My Opinion Unwarranted

Much has and will be written about the conduct of the past four years of the White house occupant from mid-January, 2017 to similar period, 2021. The stories and related details, whether factual or not, filled columns of newsprint and providing the carefully coiffured young women gracing the news sets on television channels, or their male colleagues looking more like stand in models for the latest `Gentleman's Quarterly", scripts in hand to follow, credible or not. Many have authored works which catalogued the faults and flaws in the then incumbent's past and mirroring his many statements and actions as well as numerous prior imbroglios. It is not this writer's intent to deny the accuracy of such reports and an analyses, many merely repeated what I'd read and assumed had a degree of truth. Others were patently fabricated as anyone above past the acumen of an incarcerated imbecile would recognize as flights of biased hypocrisy.

What follows within these pages is on my part a measure of theory and a compilation of my personal observations. Empirical to a degree, yet more a crocheted fabric based solely on the personal experiences and observations of the writer. It will refer directly to the corollary activity that took place during the 2020 Presidential election campaign. In addition, a personal study of study in 2016 involving the trail of pre-nomination candidate debates, the actual campaign itself and the revealing mathematics of both the electoral vote and the critical voter areas. This writer felt at the very eve of the election date that the race would be exasperating close or that Trump might, just possibly, squeak out a surprising upset. However, the earlier Von Clausewitz contention as to planning seemed to bear great relevance.

Not having voted for Trump then or not this time either, I was also unable to vote for the earlier candidate, Hillary Clinton. An individual I found to be a resident in the abyss of corrupt nature and actionable misconduct while holding previous positions. And as to the latest candidate, I had no major qualms about Joseph Biden. But, it was the crowd of conspicuous political misfits and power obsessed he was being forced to associate with that required me to once more find the name of one of the candidates in one of the lesser, unknown parties. I had the great desire to not lose my right as an American citizen vote. I found the past occupant of the Oval Office and his many tweets and sudden verbal outbursts, unbecoming the expected image of the leader of the most powerful nation in the world. A continuing era of his jabs and barbs at anyone openly in disagreement, created an often tawdry spectacle that further concerned our global partners over what seemed to be continuing national disharmony in our country.

With the evident dishevelment of common sense by both parties, any reasonable advance conjecture about the future would remain shrouded by events or situations that were not expected. A resounding discord of conflicting polls also proved the obvious failings of both candidates. Yet, it was the voter who made the final decision, although clouded and too often infected by the never ending assaults by the media. Not to omit the often unexplained disclosures and revelations of accused improper or viably illegal actions within the Trump administration, whether factual or not, engendered more public doubt and less verification during the discordant 2016 campaign and later Trump's tenure. This darkening shadow of possible corruption within the highest levels of certain government agencies then and ostensibly continuing today is a topic I will address later.

The Democratic debate presentation in mid-2020 was an unimaginable farce. A charade, as once again, much as their Republican adversaries did in 2016, a group of adults stood on the dais, literally screaming insults, unsubstantiated accusations, doing nothing to embolden their own resumes and likability. Much like a group of preschool children on a playground, lacking parental control or training, issuing caustic ridicule and gibes at one another. Most aiming their verbal venom at the former Vice President who responded much in the style of a confused contestant on one of television's ubiquitous game shows. The viewing audience had to have been confused at the vitriol issued by most of the other candidates and the almost somnolent posture of Joe Biden.

Regardless of the electoral outcome and the victory of the Democratic candidates, the writer still feels there are aspects of this political cat fight that needs airing. Actions on both sides that materially affected either side of the results but still impregnated wrongly, errors of opinion in the voting public and both parties and their constituent leadership with the stain of inconclusiveness, impropriety of action and glaring lack of constituent concern. This formed doubts that will shadow both political groups in the preparation for the 2022 midterm and 2024 presidential and major local races. So let us begin this trek among the rubble of a failed attempt to once again unify the American public

In my opinion the Democratic Party made one huge mistake regarding the nature of their opponent early on in preparation for the 2016 campaign. When Trump issued one of his numerous tweets or public comments considered by his critics as outrageous and beyond his right, the opposition, without delay, using a modern term, went *ballistic.* They immediately took to microphone and TV cameras, always available, to the casual observer, appeared to rant and rave on without pause. Demanding time easily allowed them on morning and weekend channel news programs, they decried, often near hysterically and often without definitive content, regardless whatever Trump had said or even hinted as undertaking. This continued throughout his term in office.

Their instant rebuttals became, during his four years in office,, became near histrionic condemnation to the degree it became to many viewers and listeners, a disgorging of personal hate not merely disagreement on point or principle. It provided inches of column space and many photo ops for primetime TV offering. Their combined rage automatically renewed their demand for his immediate removal and censure and contending it marked his unfitness for the position. One target, one aim and a constant barrage of denunciation. It was unparalleled since the early days of Abraham Lincoln's nomination and his period of presidency.

The Democratic Party leadership and their accommodating media colleagues refused to restrain their immediate and often vitriolic response, equally spurning, perhaps a more professional and moderate demeanor in their replies sans the constant war of words. To some observers, these sudden outbursts would seem more an irrational retort, much like children on a playground yelling back at taunts or challenges by others. The Hollywood celebrity coterie then became contributors in a battle not exactly their venue. Exhibiting public positions and advocate persona to become a cacophony of demands for his removal by whatever means, using their supposed stardom as a major political force. It failed to be effective then and unless the tabloids and other TV entertainment aficionados suddenly become respected icons of true news value, it never will.

However, this writer wishes to interject anther concept. Having read several books regarding President Donald J. Trump, one of which he ostensibly authored himself, a salient factor immediately appears evident. From the moment Trump and his wife moved down that escalator at Trump Tower to announce to the waiting media his intent to be an active contender for the presidential nomination, the assault began. The publicly expressed hatred by the Democratic Party, the gasp from the ultra-conservative leadership wing of the Republican Part and of course the total denial of him as a potential candidate by a notably biased media on behalf of the supposed anointed successor, Hillary Rodham Clinton to the sitting president, Barack Hussein Obama. This description of his entry into the 2016 political foray is not a supportive paean but rather facts. The fact borne out by the immediate verbal and TV issued criticisms from one side of the aisle and a small coterie of establishment Republicans coupled with the proven bias of much of the media over the past decades.

Trump had become quite successful in his chosen field of real estate management and development in various parts of this country and globally. He was notoriously aggressive and considered less than scrupled real estate mogul.

His various interests rank in the multi millions of dollars including hotels, realty investments, resorts and golf courses domestically and abroad. His critics quickly pointed to his numerous bankruptcies and other fiscal miscues, fully documented but still allowing him to remain one of the better known and resourceful members of his industry. Additionally, an element of his career, well understood inside the industry but never that broadly considered political analysts, was his approach to conflict.

To those who knew him, and particularly met him in the arena of business negotiations, he was was ruthless and handled many situations with a never ending and dominating combativeness when his initial requests or offerings or solicitations had been rebuffed or contested. This led to innumerable clashes with others in the realty development and finance field as well as local, state and federal officials involved in any of his undertakings. Mild mannered or complacent, quick to compromise was not part of his lexicon according to the knowledgeable people around him. And once on the campaign trail and seated in the Oval office, that natural tendency to do battle did not disappear. This was the Donald Trump both the Democratic Party, the Republicans and the media had inadvertently passed over.

The Democratically controlled media, and various political gurus kept referring to Trump as an outsider. Perhaps in their particular definition of who was an insider was merely someone outside their created domain? What they avoided addressing was that this outsider was to a great number of potential voters, well known. Not as a political name as such but easily recognized by many in the general public. Yet, in 1987 he'd joined the "Reform Party", almost becoming their candidate in the 2000 election campaign. His television program, the "Apprentice" and ownership involvement in several of the major beauty pageants made him a veritable household word. As early as the late 1980s', the Trump name was a constant aside or reference in many TV crime dramas originating out of New York City and often part of dialogue or joke lines for standup routines or hosted comedic TV offerings.

Unknown, doubtful, but perhaps only to the established political leadership - or possibly just ignored by them. This lack of knowing and attempting to understand this newcomer was an error in planning and knowledge of the competition that would come back to haunt them in 2016 and almost caused their failure in 2020. As to his past indiscretions, various romantic relationships, marriages and his noted proclivity to promoting his personal and business image, along with verbal gaffes and often acrimonious vitriolic response to critics and opponents, I leave that critique to others.

The offhanded references by others and his own public appearances since the mid-eighties, formed a public presence much greater than the Democratic hierarchy recognized in 2016 and still paid too little attention to in 2020. However, my intent is just to present a basic concept of why the current broadly held opinion that Trump defeated himself through his rather erratic and boastful nature may be true. But, then again, could be merely the image he may purposely attempted to purvey to garner the maximum public attention. Regardless of its eventual effect on his reelection bid, it was Trump in his rawest and traditional form. An individual sure of his ability to overcome whatever obstacles might be thrown in his way to achieving whatever goal piqued his interest at the time. A strong will but perhaps too rough in its application to a voter public more attuned to a less vulgar form.

As to his mental stability or his well-publicized semantic `tweet' transmitted outbursts and vigorous condemnations of who opposes him, not being a part of the psychiatric profession, I leave those considerations to those skilled in the complexity of the human psyche. I found his approach to such situations disturbing because they do not in my personal opinion reflect well on an individual in a position considered by many as the most powerful in the world. Still, there were those who felt Joe Biden exhibited lack of cogent thought, verbal difficulties and a sense of *possible* diminishing mental acuity, a failing if preparing to lead such the potentially most power laden resource in the world. That again I leave up the the experts. And having myself reached a milestone of age somewhat in advance of his, I'm not in a position to comment. What I do feel personally is the deleterious effect his encroaching coterie of fellow party notables, Nancy Pelosi, Chuck Schumer, his new VP selection, Kamala Harris coupled with the excessively verbose novice political entry, Alexandra Ocasio Cortez, all of whose intimidating ambitions for greater power are sure to become Biden's administrative millstone.

Is it possible Trump's most rabid critics may have failed to recognize this innate attitude, his aggressive nature and outward show of belligerence at any resistance that has invariably has always brought on his type of counter attack? That what they thought was merely a lack of personal control and aplomb is actually the way he always dealt with potential or ensuing conflict regarding any proposed project or undertaking? Furthermore, this sometimes bellicose approach might be designed to aggravate the opposing political entities, irritate them and create an instant need by them to retaliate by action or speech which has proven less effective with each occurrence. It was his form of combat technique in the world where such behavior may have been little noticed – rather an accepted way of entering the larger real estate development marketplace.

And so he entered the 2020 campaign, wavering not a bit from his former pugnacious and self-assertive nature. The opposition forces, absent the competing nominee, Joe Biden, instantly took to the TV microphone and helped fill columns of headlines in the print media with condemnatory statements and accusations of wrongdoing. We will always have among us those onlookers and non-allied observers who relish seeing someone telling someone else in power, basically where to go and what to do, phrasing the comment in a less prurient manner.

When months of Congressional inactivity had failed to produce any substantive law or regulatory output, this creates the image of an inactive legislature. One apparently dominated by issuing complaints and vehement response to any objectors with little or any clear or significant progress in dealing with the proclaimed problems targeting the president and/or his White House staff. When preparing to present one's accusations and definitive personal attack measures to vilify the incumbent president, it appeared much of the time was absorbed in the majority party's attempt to impeach him, failing in the Senate required trial for removal.

As a suggestion from this writer, just a private citizen, when such outbursts or debatable comments or actions or references emanate from the Oval Office, would it not have been better for the Democratic Party leadership to reconsider their response mechanism used in 2016. To be more palatable to the senses of the general public, to be recognized as a mature group, determined to maintain the expected high level of ethical and articulate nature of an august Congressional body. Simply, to hopefully exercise a degree of decorum and agreed protocol in such matters? Among Trump's more notable detractors, his niece, daughter of his brother who himself had emotional problems. She wrote a vicious denigration of her uncle filled with her condemnation of him both as a person and someone unfit to be in his position.

However, as with all such volumes emerging from some undisclosed venom, one will have to make their own decision as to the books overall verity. The other book producing disparager, once a member of the president's principal staff, had himself lofty ambitions according to those in the know and his particular effort was more a literary whining than factual presentation. With all such deprecators, belittlement too often replaces factual recitation and the appropriate opinion of such events whether positive or negative. Trump's vilifying niece and the insipidity of former state department minion, John Bolton, did little but harvest personal book publishing income. To many, it may have had some revelatory value but little in political nuance or substantive commentary.

During these heated ripostes by Democratic and media spokespersons, had not they been more limited, more refined in texture, more in keeping with the demeanor of someone confident of their position and desirous of maintain a high level of professionalism? It might be better to present an air of disregard of many of contended inflammatory statements by Trump. Immobilizing their public effect of his comments with quiet statements recognizing the right of others to speak their mind but disagreeing in a composed, articulate manner? Responding to whatever had been posed or threatened by the President in a manner presenting a professionally calm and self-confident manner. Should this not be the manner we expect of our elected representatives?

It is my opinion Trump could have purposely attempted to throw the Democratic leadership off their intended game. He appeared to use this offensive strategy in 2016 and may he decided to envelop his competitors in the same emotional net any wise aggressor in combat desires, to utilize in order to confuse and agitate the opposition to become frustrated and thus, indecisive as to a proper retort. He would force indecision into their thinking, creating the inability of the opponent to calmly consider their next move and how to deal with a sudden and unexpected thrust by the adversary. When one is first encompassed by an immediate anger and desires to instantly reply or attack without plan, the battle is soon lost and the observers know that the outcome may soon be decided.

While the Democratic Party and its faithful adherents were banging on the doors of the White House demanding their turn to enter and take residency, Trump was out campaigning. When finally Biden left his basement location and faced the voters on a greatly limited and almost insecure approach in presenting his positions, of the issues facing the voters, he may have been considered weak and ineffective as a forceful campaigner by many. It's a plausible assumption that the emerging pandemic his supporters felt he wished to avoid was in actuality a desire and need to avoid continual response to the bombastic Trump output.

In what seemed rather constricted replies, Biden appeared to agree with stronger part of the new Democratic Party's liberal wing social, economic and political reforms, regardless of their potential cost as was claimed by the opposition. His sometimes timidity, and tenuous approach, along with verbal gaffes' and a degree of factual uncertainty brought forward questions as to his actual intents as president, which would have been in defiance to pressures being leveraged by the progressive advocates. It still has not been conclusively proven that the near ludicrous nature of a number of Biden's earlier and later affirmed proposals are actually his per se, or merely the dictated objectives of the shadow core of the socialist oriented left wing of the Democratic party.

For many, there arose the perception that the current party in control of the House of Representatives had had the power and responsibility to accomplish numerous similar proposals but failed in attending to such matters. Rather, spending a majority of its time in constant battle with the incumbent. Is it feasible that their lack of close attention to the current needs and in many cases the will of the people might be separating them somewhat from the reality of all election campaigning and vote solicitation per a number of observers? Determining what the voter wants, articulating it in a clear and decisive manner evoking confidence to follow through with those promises is what the voter expects. Failing this responsibility they did oust the incumbent but still failed to gain the confidence of the general public and suffering a smaller majority in the House.

On the other hand, the national senatorial race in Georgia put two temporarily installed individuals in those, vacated prior to completion of the incumbent's term, against two new entries. The nature of the competition had potentially graver consequences for both parties. One Democratic hopeful, young, considered of the nouveau liberal youth movement. The other, a local African American religious figure whose background resounded with numerous criticisms of the government and somewhat dubious praise for less than equally heroic figures, such as Fidel Castro. The runoff election for both positions, scheduled for January 5, 2020, eventually gave created an even split in the Senate thus providing the Democratic Party the ability to acquire the simple majority of one vote through the Constitutional provision of the Vice president casting any deciding vote. It could later determine the ability or lack thereof for the Democrats to move their future agenda through a revised Senate majority. Although, in certain legislative decision, the existing filibuster rule still gave the Republican voice in the Senate virtual prohibition of any measure requiring sixty votes as against the normal simple majority.

Severely hampering the Republican program to delay the opposition's liberal advance, both Democratic candidates won with a financial expenditure by both sides escalating to ridiculous and ethically obscene heights. With their victory the Senate now stood at fifty Democrats and 50 Republicans, bringing cheer to the ultra-liberal contingent, and as mentioned, the use of the incoming Vice President's vote. It is apparent the Democrats avoided a majority blocking control by the opposition which would have hampered both incoming President Biden and the progressive wing of his party from achieving at least a portion of their liberal legislative efforts. Still, bickering on Senate rules and the possibility that the newly installed Senate majority leader, Charles Schumer, might not be able to totally control his party colleagues during highly controversial legislative considerations, the "filibuster factor" became the primary target of Democrats. Removing it would allow a veritable open road for movement through the Senate, House engendered liberal legislation regardless of Republican opposition.

In reviewing the tactics undertaken by Trump as he prepared for his clash with Biden to gain his reelection, could he have once again been luring the Democratic Party into the miasma of self-doubt and inconsequential mumbling, they appearing voiceless to the voter's demand for answers to the questions and dilemmas facing us all? When the official campaign period began, the question among political observers was who shall be the dominant image on the trail of potential voters? All those with a big "D" next to their name are normally committed. To the right, "the equally big "R" next to a large contingent who may likely remain supporters of the incumbent.

Yet, it was still supposed that independent voters would be subject to both candidate's vigorous campaign to secure those votes as that supposedly remains the determining factor in every election. We have become a nation of less dogmatic approval of one side or another, rather than becoming our own, individual decision makers. One needs to remember those who surprisingly switched from the lethargic, policy bereft, Hillary Clinton campaign to the indecipherable and visually aggressive Donald Trump. She assumed the nature of his supporters. He gauged the effect of her campaign lethargy and she discarded the level of his dedicated energy.

Regardless of the need to move into the new presidency in a relatively smooth manner, it was again the politically brash and combative newcomer who with all honesty, despite one's political leaning, entered the political campaign arena once more like the proverbial bull in the staid china shop. Over the past four year term, undoubtedly the controversial New York realtor became far less appealing and now an increased target for his eventual removal. In doing, was it just that the majority of voters moved toward the kindly imaged Joe Biden with his fifty year career on the national scene? Or was the choice far less disturbing to the average citizen. In 2016 there were many indicators being adjudged by both mathematical and physical computation. Today, the decision in the minds of many during 2020 was probably made long before this essay would ever see light.

As a result, the unchanging fiery Trump rhetoric and constant, irritating use of the tweet commentary system changed the direction of numerous voters who may have considered his previous successes reason for extending his tenure another four years. However, and again, as said earlier, this once seemingly successful 2016 strategy from the 45th President, but exacerbated by his increasing erratic behavior, failed to market a saleable product to the voting public.

Although having garnered, over 74 million votes, far more than any other losing candidate, he still faltered almost five million votes behind the winner. To his critics it indicated the overwhelming desire of his opponents to effect the change they've long felt was required. The acrimonious nature of the recent election campaign and following accusations of corruption and fraud will long be remembered as it affected both sides of the struggle. It might be of value for both candidates to remember the `Lygian' fable, wherein, "An eagle, flying aloft, was struck by an arrow. When looking at its feathered shaft, said to himself, truly, it is by ourselves we are slain and not others."

As calculated by his supporters, the media and academic milieu, his remaining and impressive number of avid followers may still provide him a continuing and potentially dominant public image in his future undertakings. To paraphrase one of Dylan Thomas' best known phrases, it is felt by many that Donald J. Trump will not "go gentle into that good night." He may have taken a quote from an actor, Arnold Schwarzenegger movie, declaring, "I'll be back." Only time and the machinations of political and legal entanglement will determine his immediate future. However, he could suffer the same fate as others of major public presence. Either disliked or revered, with passing time and other more consequential events and public trauma, he could well fade into the fog of anonymity faced by similar predecessors.

I may be considered negligent by his supporters if I avoided any mention, however slight, of his accomplishments which were emblematic of his strong push to achieve regardless of the opposition. However, before being declared an apologist for him, I will leave any extolling of any of Trump's achievements to his avid constituency. As for for the constant claim that he lacked traditional presidential composure and controlled displays of temperament, I will assign that task to his rabid critics to expound upon.

It would be remiss of the writer, based on current information and undoubtedly to be part of the history of this period, there were those overt acts and undertakings by various members of the Democratic hierarchy and again, secretly, even those in Trump's own party to unseat him. Most regrettable was the revelations of the actual interference by the FBI and other government agencies to participate in similar actions to remove or curtail the authority of the president. As is always the case, the truth and full documentation of such conduct will be buried in the archives and when eventually fully disclosed will, regrettably greaten the blemish on a once vaunted law enforcement body. Their apparent politicizing of certain actions, coupled with the incessant media barrage regardless of fact, will have cheapened the image they enjoyed for so many years. This was a violation of their oath.

The one continuing aspect of much of the commentary by his most ardent faultfinders was the use of language, in the most part incendiary in nature and either libelous or slanderous were it not for the vaunted forgiveness of the First Amendment of the Constitution. The social media giant, Facebook comments were laced with obscenity and the vilest descriptive profanity. Although they continued without restraint, I noted at least a half dozen other Facebook habitués complaining that their kindred and improper use of the English language were constantly removed by the Facebook service soon after appearing.

An interesting symptom of systemic censorship which I leave to others to discuss. While Trump exhibited his own voraciously livid style of commentary, figures on the opposite side were equally at fault for a dialogue that would be more at home among a group of riotous drunkards than supposedly distinguished members of Congress. They must share the public's disdain for such immature behavior. It seemed that Trump's approach was so aggravating to their establishment mental set, their hostility formed a fog of hate - venomous hate. Sad when that emotion becomes a primary source for the vernacular of those we entrust with our government's future.

The protection granted legislators, other government officials and the media in the First Amendment is not unassailable. It has limits, but too often construed in a manner that defends the offender and leaves the recipients without reasonable challenge. In this writer's more recent book, "The Faultless Imperfection," this part of the US Constitution is extensively discussed. However, it is one of the cornerstones of our basic freedoms and like all foundations should not be measurably altered. The abuse of this linguistic right has become so prevalent in the Halls of Congress and throughout the media as to warrant disdain by the average citizen. It will be referred to later in this essay.

Chapter 3

Let Us Continue

Now to the primary topics comprising this endeavor. As this dissertation was being composed, two new and distinct visitors appeared on the scene that markedly affected the then upcoming election? Or radically altered the direction of this nation's traditional methods involving economics, social order and the threat or actual imminence of war both abroad and at home. Most publicly accepted spokespersons soon became clarions of potential doom or disaster and how such situations would affect the nation's future.

First, a SARS virus carrying pandemic, referred to as Coronavirus or more specifically Covid-19. It has caused innumerable deaths and at the time of this writing continues its lethal rampage. Its effect has seriously engendered forth both personal and economic havoc, forcing innumerable business closings, perhaps never to reopen. High unemployment and serious financial consequences for many Americans, especially the lesser advantaged, minority communities and still undocumented newcomers to our country. The sinews of our economic strength were being strained and weakened various areas of normal and expected commerce that have had to drastically curtail and potentially eliminate numerous services.

With its current devastating loss in lives and increasing cases of an illness that has literally limited normal human movement, the lasting effects of the Covid onslaught may not be realized for several more years. Possibly industries affected by the restrictions will seek greater technologically adaptable production methods and lesser labor costs plus avoidance of inevitable tax increases and pressure from unions, sill succumb to the lure of overseas manufacturing and distribution. And as always, the now accelerated and as always, continuing need to address the question of overall care for and attention to the absence and limitations on current medical services and assistance for the underprivileged.

The question of the virus origination will be discussed and badgered by experts and conspiracy advocates for years. Possibly developed in laboratories located in the Chinese city of Wuhan, a created resource in some type bio warfare research by the Chinese military. Or, as some contend, an accidental release within the laboratory or an equally accidental relay by a single employee returning to his or her home after a day's contact with the virus? Most recently, the World health organization – WHO – has insisted it came from the iniquitous bat. Possibly understandable as there are over 1,200 bat specie in the world, China being home to approximately one hundred of the creatures. Time and eventual unbiased fact finding may tell us. Whatever the final resolution, the Covid-19 virus has become reminiscent of the horrific Spanish Flu epidemic of 1918 which decimated millions of people.

The second visitor to the year 2020 was a continuing plague of protests soon turned into the constant occasions for rioting, destruction of property and damage to private businesses, intimidation, injury and death to innocent civilians and the repeated demand for dismantling, defunding or removal of traditional police law enforcement systems. This ravaging was circumstanced supposedly by the group titling itself the Black Lives Matters, for brevity sake just, BLM. A movement to create a unified voice of protest ostensibly initiated by the tragic and illegal death of an African-American by a police officer administering an unwarranted physical action that caused the man's death.

Still, it claimed to be an outraged public's call for justice and correction of accused past police iniquity, yet the question exists. There had been a history over the years of improper law enforcement use of unauthorized procedures, outright physical excess against black and other minority suspects or transients. The record revealed incompetent police leadership, violation of the basic rights of all citizens and an equal lack of supervision by the courts and prosecutors assigned such incidents. As a result, numerous other such police involved arrests, shootings and wrongful physical reaction to individuals being stopped and questioned, revealed a litany of abuse that needed correction and reformation nationwide. As expected, it became the battle cry of the activist, the bane of police administration and the fodder of local political oriented administrations.

The question of who was the hierarchy of the Black Lives matters organization, funding source? And most important, who determined that the incurring violence, destruction, threats and assaults on those not involved with their efforts was a justifiable method of protest? The massive number of continuing protests became nightly rages of burned out businesses, assaults on security and police attempting to quell the increasing crowd sizes. Deaths of innocent bystanders occurred, both local residents and various government principals were threatened. The nation experienced a daily siege of such protests in many American cities leading to an immediate divergence of opinion as to the rights of the protestors and the need to control the ensuing violence.

The initial incident that supposedly ignited the vast number of claimed earlier such acts by police officer and later misuses of physical restraint including shootings, supposedly highlighted a history of serious flaws in many police departments. Occurring in the city of Minneapolis in May of 2020, the incident involved an improper method of restraint by a police office on the neck of of a handcuffed black suspect. As a result, the individual died and it was determined that not only unauthorized by normal procedure, the officer's knee on the individual's neck was the primary cause for his death. What occurred was the impetus for a continuous series of violent protests against what was claimed to be systematic racism in police departments throughout the country.

What happened at that time and both earlier and later situations involving officer involved shootings and disputed arrest tactics, garnered automatic support from both political and social activists. Claimed was inadequate training procedures and the argued defect in police candidate selection process. It was these primary situations that protest leaders and eventually supportive national and local legislative officials joined in a demand for reformation of all police policies and practices. Demand then rose to reduce police funding, to utilize non-armed, social worker oriented replacements to deal with numerous types of 911 emergency calls. This ostensibly was to create better relationships with sensitive community cultural differences and material changes in police arrest and restraint procedures.

An inquiry also arose as to the nature of BLM and allied organizations and funding sources that seemingly controlled the protests. The shift in opinion as to the incessant extent of what was considered a viable and justified protest cause may have seriously affected both political parties in their campaign approaches. Scenes of brutal reaction brought into each and every home via the ever present TV news channel and growing profusion of cell phone cameras, has, in the opinion of some, aggravated unnecessarily the insistence of some groups to continue their violent, public demonstrations in excess of the rights embedded in the First Amendment.

The complete story as to the original founding of the Black Lives Matters movement, its core organization and particularly its as yet unidentified funding sources, forced local authorities to face an unknown antagonist. One that critics claimed was devoid of interest in compromise or moderation to pursue their goals. It these very goals and objectives that concern many. Ostensibly, the main objective of the general protest was declared as possible total dismantling of all police forces, measurable defunding of local police operations and the implementation of "incident intervention specialists" instead of armed police officers. Without such immediate moves to satisfy the proposed protest demands, the threat of increasing anti-police movements would continue. To many it was the time to reform past law enforcement methods and procedures. To others, moves to defund police, restrict their movements and replace them with social workers to handle certain service calls it, presented an ever present jeopardy to the very foundation of the current governance and freedom of action enjoyed by law enforcement.

Our history is ostensibly being cleansed by what the Black Lives Matters and its corollary ultra-liberal and progressive sycophants who declared past ills and police irresponsibility was salient reasoning for wholescale public disorder caused by the increasing protest violence. With rioting, looting, firebombing, destruction of private property, intimidation and injury to private citizens coupled with assaults on police, including throwing of rocks, bottles and carrying of weapons resulted in injury to numerous police present. It became apparent the nature of the protest format did little more than exhibit hate rather than just cause.

The heralded emblems of the evil practice of slavery that in any manner identified or were part of the disastrous Civil War, are being removed, destroyed and vandalized. Notably, in the protest crowd's agitator generated rage, even the images of those who history reports were active abolitionists and violently opposed to slavery, even during its greatest prevalence in our society have suffered the wrath of ignorant mobs. Statues, portraits and memorials featuring the previous military and political leadership of the former Confederate States, have been destroyed in some emotional display of rebuking a history, however sad and rife with injustice. That history still remains part of the national archives containing our past, however glorious or distasteful is being sublimated by the anger of the mob is real or fomented.

This pathologically generated carnage often seems supported and acquiesced by local political leaders and municipal officials who fear the mob mentality threatens their hold on administrative power or future at the voting booths. There seems to be this constant rush to rewrite history, yet those arguing such actions seem to forget that the difficulty lies in the fact that history will just keep happening regardless of our efforts to interpret and understand what is and has happened.

Allowing uncontrolled and little argument against such riotous displays is cowardice at its most venal level. The protection of the citizenry and the enhancement of the atmosphere in which its constituency can function and enjoy the freedoms and opportunities offered by the Constitution is the primary obligation of these elected and appointed officials. To avoid or minimize response to the devastation, both physical and socially committed by the core elements of such protests is a violation of their oath of office. Contrary to the intent of such groups to raise the level of acceptance of their demand for reform and major reconstruction of society and the insistence for increased diversity, a storm is brewing on the horizon. Not an impending maelstrom of public support that will vindicate and remove from memory the destruction, firebombing, looting and deaths incurred during multiple public protests, rather a silent contravention of the BLM's primary goals. Eventually a potentially volatile resistance to the proliferation of certain demands related to ultimatums to either defund or in certain instances, eliminate the present police forces and their mission of public security.

In this writer's opinion, one it feels is shared by many, the nucleus of the BLM movement, along with its nebulous and somewhat suspicious association with the `Antifa' group, is not simply reformation of police procedures or the needed increased awareness by all concerned of racial, cultural and community sensibilities. More simply it is an effort to achieve revision of specific portions of our current governmental structure. By avoiding constitutional processes for changes to the Constitution itself, the group and its funding and ideological resource s could be empowered to institute operational and legislative agendas that could in fact, veritably reduce the US Constitution to parchment sheets of insignificant notes by our Founding Fathers.

This proposed method of change would no longer be the form of government, unheralded in the history of mankind with its direct application of rights and permissions. Rather, a document to be altered, interpreted and legislatively abused by the political structure in power. This use of an originally sincere and constitutionally allowed method of bringing attention to the lack of diversity regarding many areas of social, economic and legal process has potentially created an undeniable thrust by unknown entities to alter fundamentally the structure of our governing system. It was in the beginning, ostensibly a noble action to bring reason to an untenable law enforcement lack of an effective minority community relationship that has been twisted into personal machinations by a heretofore indistinguishable segment intent of their own revolutionary goals and objectives.

We are also facing the newest demands to free our personal and historic ties to various attributes of our past supposedly found offensive by a moral hierarchy yet identified. The insistence that all sports teams, schools and other groups, publicly financed or not, be required to change their designation as reflected in their logo, brand image or actual name to assure no other indigenous, minority or special interest body could or might be offended. Further to allow athletes to have social dialogue, position statements and politically correct slogans on the backs of their uniforms may bring cheers to advocates but can also further alienate a public still in dismay over such activities. The total allowance of sports team owners and school administrators to personal opinions to be reflected at all sports events by the kneeling or holding up of an arm in what is considered by some as the defiance of the current social status.

There arose a proposal that new texts be created espousing the ideology of the BLM and its associated coterie, however extreme, for all middle and high school level grades. Academic courses requiring all incoming freshmen at larger educational institutions to attend specific instruction on the "evils of white control," and a disdain for wealth and position. That is other than the celebrity levels of the sports and entertainment industry. Additionally to recognize the need to automatically guarantee economic and positional equality be a requisite regardless of training, education, skill level or even lack of exhibited effort to succeed. Where once it was the struggle against the age old perversion of segregation and violation of the black man's civil rights and abuse of minorities that garnered increased public support, the new outrage espoused by the new progressive and ultra-liberal mentality was "white privilege.

Children were to be taught to condemn their own non-minority ethnicity, to feel they must repent for the evils of their white parents and youthful associates. One example of this, at times, ridiculous and mentally superfluous thinking is the current suggestion, fortunately not apparently gaining support that the University of Utah, a major participant in the national collegiate scene and honored member of the academic world should change their sports team logo and name "Utes." The Utes, a relatively small American Indian tribe and family by population, not as well known or publicized over the years in literature, history, movies or television as the Apache, Comanche, Sioux, still, were original residents of the Utah area for which the state was named.

Other than being an important part of the paleontological and Indian cultural archives, criticized by certain groups as to the university's use of the name regardless of their ongoing contributions to the tribe, fiscally and educationally to their betterment and public awareness of this unique part of American history. This mode of mental misdirection was part of the overall effort to remove any supposed sports team image that might, to whatever minimal degree, the sensitivities of some ethnic culture supposedly being represented.

This indecisive dialogue by ideologically mutant state officials has also crept into the Utah educational system, related to the various indigenous American Indian names or references utilized by many of the high schools. A state, developed when the Indian was the primary resident, the progenitor of what culture existed when the early hunters and fortune seekers entered, is now to be divested of what remains in the honoring of our early residents. The expression Braves, "Redman", or whatever ancient tribe populated the area before the entry of the supposed civilized interloper are now considered racists. Again, the obvious use of a word that can be interpreted in many variations, only to become the demanded mantra of the avowed ultra-liberal legislative back slappers.

The indigenous American is a proud symbol of the early inhabitants of this beautiful state. I wonder if our mission misguided members of the educational system and legislatures have ever spent the time to direct all required decisions to the leadership of any and all local or assimilated tribes. They are the ones who should speak for their constituency, not the headline seekers and photo op collectors.

The demand that language commonly used for decades, be sanitized of those verbiages that have, could or may offend some other group or individual has become the mantra of the revisionist cadre. Or as the writer George Orwell so vividly described in his famous novel, "1984", as "newspeak." The elimination of the SAT scoring system to determine the minimum educational qualifications for college entry so as to assure anyone can apply for institutions of higher education regardless of their possible total inability to deal with the least difficult subject matter to be experienced in such institutions. Furthermore, that the control of all educational processes, regulations and administration be placed in the hands of government as overseen by selected members of activist groups to assure their doctrine is meticulously followed.

That access to higher education should be at the cost of government which in due transition, payment by the taxpayer body. The more elite universities had demanded that restrictions on foreign student visas be eliminated as the American college system is still the most desired in the world. That it provides a bountiful financial benefit to such schools regardless of from where comes the students or their potentially radical viewpoints. Today, another academic swing as certain ethnicities, primarily Asian and Indian, appear to lead in the development of scholar students and later achieving measurable success in their chosen field. Viewpoints of these young people from areas besieged by the difficulties of lack of personal freedoms, can in the minds of more ultra-liberal academics reduce the influence of the Marxists oriented leftists instructional intent. But then, let us leave the culturally abridged indoctrination of our collegiate population for another time.

The demand that the national anthem, the American flag, the display of religious symbols that may allegedly offend other groups, atheists, anarchists and the rare non connected Islamic radical element, should be either drastically changed in appearance or eliminated so as to assure diversity without insult. This "taking offense" is what may become the spark that will ignite a violent reaction by those who will meet such situations with both total disdain or if forcing confrontation, physical resistance. The continuing examples of such greatly challenged demands can best be described by a simple revelation as to its beginnings. When the tragic and uncalled for death of that black man in Minneapolis by police using totally unacceptable physical restraint, occurred, a massive hue and cry arose, generating destructive, community debilitating and legally irresponsible protests. The police were immediately accused as the reason for any dissension or disparate action by the inhabitants of the neighborhood. Targeted was the activist claim that the Minneapolis event and those prior to and post that incident, existed because of systematic racism within most police force operations. A condemnation quickly supported verbally and in print by local political and municipal officials.

The recognized degree of police lack of diversity, insensitivity and disrespect for minority culture is contended as the basis for all the brutal occurrences and inappropriate law enforcement responses over the years. Their conduct must be brought to order regarding transgressions against the rights of the black man and any minority individual or group – agreed in whole – but somewhat convoluted in the proposed methods of reforming a past filled with racial inequities and lack of appropriate restraint during altercations of any nature. We of the general public have assented to the need for marked change in minority relations and police procedural conduct. In this writers opinion, that immediate acquiescence did not countenance the following days of violence, injury, death, intimidation of private citizens and destruction of businesses to allow criminal for looting and extensive theft.

All seemed well and good with the public desire to arouse wider awareness of the problems and needs with constitutionally guaranteed protest action. That was until the political pawns of the progressive movement, the vote hungry national and local politician and other once aggrieved but later forgotten entities joined in on the outcries. It was then the potential insurrectionist element felt enabled. They had found a ready vehicle to pursue their goals and objectives. The initial guileless crowd was the ideal setting for the particular form of assault on both government controlled and civilian enterprises desired by the provocateurs. The nightly gathering of diverse participants was the perfect opportunity for trained agitators to enter the main protest body, basically melding in with those who honestly believed that raising their voices and demanding attention to the problems faced by minorities and difficulties with law enforcement and needing immediate resolution.

What always seems missing from these messages of absolutism, was who was at fault for the violence present at almost all such demonstrations. Absent appeared to be one of the major focal points in the nature of such gatherings, possibly that of a diminished parental obligation to counsel their children on the most prudent method to conduct oneself when encountering a questioning police officer or being the target of an inquiry – however brief or non-accusatory. Unless of course, fleeing from participation in illegal activity – just simple logic. The continual debasement of "the man" as police officers are too often categorized in minority neighborhoods has created the automatic disdain for any type of legal and necessary security and law enforcement. Again, a philosophy or contended fact too often relayed from parent or associate to the child emerging into adulthood.

Yes, quantitative and qualitative readjustment of numerous police procedures need to be reexamined and all the necessary changes made – and very soon. That will also be discussed later. In addition, the right of the teacher to be another dominant influence and holder of the role of reasonable discipline when challenged or threatened has been abrogated by the ever present ACLU and an ever burgeoning teacher's union. Litigation has replaced lesson planning and demonstrations for ill-defined youth rights has set aside the original role of the teacher and school administrator. I n the domain of higher education, it is the power of administrative councils, the power of the highest financial donor and the interference of academic cabals that have taken control of both the curricula and usefulness of the individual institution in providing a free flow of opinion regardless of the speaker or subject.

Allow me to digress for a moment and further reexamine this entire crowd syndrome, seemingly avoided by both the reporting media and the confluence of social pundits eager to explain the outrage ostensibly being demonstrated by these protest groups. I've written in earlier digests on what I have long considered to the forgotten aspect of any large crowd whether it be a gathering at some preplanned or incidental event or as formed for a protest purpose. It is this core concept we shall now, with your permission by continuing your reading, review to a much greater extent. I will present my findings from experience and what I've observed over the years in a first person format. I've entitled it, "A crowd of familiar faces." The current focal point of my observations and comment is the downtown area of Salt Lake City, Utah. Known as a relatively conservative urban area facing mostly those incidents and public disruptions common to a city of its size.

As a preface, a bit of previous history please. For weeks since the Minneapolis death of George Floyd, a black man, reportedly caused by an inappropriate action by one or more police officers, I've viewed scene after scene on television news channels of the raging protests ostensibly stemming from that illegal action in late May, 2020. Aside from the details of that brutal reaction by a sworn police office, his almost immediate firing and later charged at first with Third Degree Murder, still to be determined later and his companion officers at the scene also now being reviewed for serious criminal charges, Further comment I leave to the various media formats and the ersatz pundits television insists on employing.

What struck me most strikingly, watching the almost seven hours of televised protest action in my own Salt Lake City downtown area, bordered by the relatively new police station and architecturally magnificent library building, was automobiles being turned over, fires set, and police officers being pelted with water bottles, rocks and pieces of debris from the varied acts of destruction and damage to local business. Perhaps not as violent as the Minneapolis, New York,

Philadelphia, Baltimore, Portland, OR, Washington, DC and similar but more aggressive nightly happenings in large urban centers was its almost surreal nature. It appeared an oddity as the Salt Lake community is dominated by the ideology, legislative and judicial control of the Church of Jesus Christ of Latter Days, better known as the LDS or `Mormons.

Although a place where grievous incidents have and will continue, as that is the nature of mankind, it is still an urban area not adapted to what would occur. Yet, the crowds present seemed more like a species, one that unlike the animal kingdom, who will kill for purposes only of seeking food or protecting its young, this new type can and will, without notice or the least apparent provocation, attack, injure and kill members of their own human kind and destroy and pillage without apparent reason of visible provocation.

Inasmuch as my view of the Salt Lake protest was graphically enabled by all the local TV outlet control of the news available and the instigating headline coverage in the local Salt Lake Tribune featuring close-ups of both the protestors and their actions, clearly defined the effect on local viewers which had to be greatly unsettling. However, on at least three occasions, one or more of the TV reporters would say that the audience should understand that what they were viewing were just protestors. Considering the burning police cars, looted store, raging fires and objects being thrown, the remarks were Pollyanna and self-serving, perhaps due to the quite young, and apparently un prepared reporters on scene. What we the viewers at home were seeing were criminal acts by those who had become thieves and arsonists and assaulters. What was needed was a closer inspection of the `core', the centralized organism that is emplaced to urge, exacerbate and increase where possible the more violent and illegal actions of any mob gathering.

From my fifty years of experience, numerous observations have indicated when a few gathered individuals will become a crowd. Urged on by those with disparate reasons, they can become a protest. Add to that the potential for physical assault and oppositional interaction, they become a mob. When the core of the group is destruction of property, riotous behavior, looting, intimidation and harm to both collateral members and innocent civilians and the use of violent response to security, they have instituted an insurrection. The Black Lives Matters protest was initially to bring to the attention of responsible authorities the need to recognize, review and correct the inadequacy and history of wrongful law enforcement relationship and evident racial bias in dealing with minority individuals and in their communities for several hundred years. Nevertheless, the destruction, the firebombing, collateral the injury and deaths of participants, the flagrant plundering of private businesses has to stop. It has regrettably provided a large segment of the American viewer an image of self-emolument and aggrandizement by those who had supposedly desired only the ". . . right to peaceably assemble, and to petition the government for a redress of grievances."

Chapter 4

A Past Too Well Remembered

After several hours of watching the particular protests in Salt Lake City where I live, I realized I was not looking at strangers but rather, familiar faces. Not people I knew personally or among whom I dwelled with in our neighborhood. Instead, a vivid memory of those thousands of faces that populated those hundreds of large concert, sports or convention events during my 45-year career in major facility management and international sports event operation That and my three years of direct involvement in the patron operations in major league baseball and professional soccer.

As I peered at the TV screen and its constantly changing scenes and up close camera angles, I could finally recognize the core of the protesting group. That nucleus that forms the heat source for most protests and can result in damaging action, violent behavior and the use of missiles, weapons and fire to implant their desire to initiate the action they, and mostly they, intended. To understand this unique aspect of group or crowd protestation, one must have had the experience of seeing such situations develop, the more serious element initiated and the instances that often create the specific propellant that gathers support for exacerbation of what, until that time, had been controllable and lacking any measurable threat.

Alcohol and drug use can be counted as initiating the irrational behavior of those lacking education or training, parental or otherwise, in controlling ones emotions. Particularly that seeming natural proclivity to be offended by actions of others they feel threatening and are always prime vehicles for the start of that rolling thunder heralding eruption of angered crowd mentality. Although, regrettably, it seems that with the appearance of television cameras and accompanying reporters, the energy source of a crowd seems to ignite that first burst of reaction hoped for and immediately utilized by that aforementioned nucleus of intended trouble makers. Is it the lure of having ones face on television so the world can see any self-endowed machismo or personality? Or to become immortalized on video tape or other electronic imagery? Or merely the planned process by the professional agitators paid to be the fulcrum from which anger and violence can be initiated? Whatever, when the media has arrived, too often personal common sense and normal restraint seem to disappear. This allows the purposeful dilettantes of destructive intent to become the spark that fires the boiling point past rational control to meaningless reaction.

Still, there are two separate types of gatherings that can create such a canvas of images. The normal collection if individuals attending an event, be it entertainment, sports or a convening of like interests form crowds, assemblages, throngs, hordes of people, depending on the viewer's interpretation of the makeup of the collection. Then there is the protest gathering. The convergence of a multitude of persons to voice their support or opposition to some act or lack thereof or particularly desired outcome. In each situation can be found the core of diverse interest. With the grouping of spectators at an event, among them are, unfortunately at times, a few whose psychological insufficiency for restraint will allow them to react to specific triggers.

Action alerts generated by the conduct or behavior of the event participants or featured attraction as in the case of certain rock music groups, very loud, physically boisterous, often adding their personal beliefs on the youthful audience in attendance can be the impulse for irrational behavior. In the domain of the modern music era, it can be those factors previously referred to, drugs, alcohol, and the closeness of overly energized beholders. These few provocateurs react only when it seems they may wish public notice of their personal ability to rebel against whatever conduct is ostensibly required at such events. And of course, there will always be the alcohol imbued fan at the baseball, basketball or other sports competition who decides to make an ass of himself, either amusing fellow attendees or becoming of a distraction to require security personnel attention. The innate bully or blusterer who never overcame their sense of inferiority in school and adapted the persona of oppressor to heighten his or her public image can unfortunately be found at many public gatherings.

In the case of the protest formation, immediately upon the development of such groups, the core of those sincerely gathered to display solidarity in their appeal for resolution of their cause have unwittingly allowed within the group core, the virus of planned and predetermined turbulence. This infection begins immediately after the initial announcement or formation of the protest group as there exist activist groups, intending only conflict. They are are prepared to immediately insert their agents into that core. When such protests continue long beyond the scheduled time frame set by the organizers, ranging into days, the core is solely in the control of the criminal intent of the disrupting element.

As the protest continues and the damage and violent repercussions are extended, the protest body itself is cloaked in a Velcro like garment, attracting every dimension of trash, criminal intent and maniacally disturbed participants. This created adhesive is the ultimate opportunity for the thief, the looter, the individual who will always, when provided the opportunity, seize what they want without payment. When the fires still rage, the looting and vandalism continues it becomes the hallmark of an unbroken plan to besiege and commit possible injury to security forces and innocent observers alike. It is this infected core that is now in total control.

In full compliance with First Amendment rights allowing full coverage of these tragic outcomes to what were originally peacefully intended gatherings, this ravaging of our cities and destruction of their economic welfare is the required staple of the news reporting industry. Unfortunately, we are now faced with a new abundance of pseudo news outlets; that growing plethora of cell phone reporters who never fail to electronically record any occurrence, however benign but might have some value when submitted to the local television outlets or headline obsessed print media. As a result, no action, no circumstance, however needing assistance rather than bystander filming, is safe from what has become the bane of objective reporting of any situation. A major concern with all these cell phone videos, how and when they were recorded. From what angle, at what distance and was the recording altered in any manner, either by the phone user or eventually when finding its way to the television production room?

During my facility management career, having hosted many events that drew a highly diverse attendance, it became important to locate the individuals, that ill-defined core you felt would be the center of any eruptive disturbance were the occasion merit its happening. There was of course, as part of the modern music field, the 'Rock & Roll" era, arose its increasingly aggressive successor, 'hard rock'. Often grossly laced with profanity, racial inference and calls for physical overthrow of the national government or whatever current protest phobia was in fashion. These events too often were the scene of such crowd reaction. However, their core was not that of the current protest group infection, rather the need to express themselves in a fashion marking their passing of the childhood age. Individuals still demanding exposition of their freedom to be different. Fortunately that previous potential has appeared to subside, the audiences at these events less intentioned for disruption. Yet, the management of the event location, be it entertainment or sports must still be ever vigilant as that core, that infection of the uncaring for the other attendees will like most viruses, always be present

As mentioned earlier, I recognized the faces of their progenitors, the same sallow faced, unkempt appearing younger generation who appeared as listless in their lack of ambition during the more histrionic youth oriented music age. You could recognize groups of younger people, eighteen to mid-twenties, possibly poverty limited, without substantive career opportunities, either shortened college involvement or even less social involvement of the positive nature. Individuals with that wanderlust look, that apparent lack of concern for anyone but their own satisfaction or comfort. There are a multitude of reasons that urges some people to gravitate and participate in protests. Perhaps a sincere desire to be part of the `*vox populi*', the natural desire to convene with others or the curiosity of the lonely and socially disappointed. I've come to believe this type attending groups can be to the malignant few an advantage to whom such protests provide the right circumstance to take advantage of their personal agenda.

It should be understood the lack of sufficient income or various educational input are not necessarily primary reasons for the creation of these core crowd inciters. More likely, paid representatives of certain special interest groups bent on using crowd's unrecognized susceptibility to skilled internal agitation are there to augment fervor of the protest itself. Trained to generate far larger response by the truly sincere individuals, continuing the yelling, slogans, and continuous demands for justice or decrying the presence of any security forces. And this requires greater security presence to forestall potential for violence or damage, needing to be be fully equipped if matters were to exceed simple shouting and banner and placard waving. In numerous cases, the crowd's sudden increase in pressure on police and security personnel present can, and unfortunately does result in inappropriate actions by security in restraining the crowd. It also allows the core activist's acts of violence, destruction of property, invasion and tooting of local business and the use of firebombs to add further fear and chaos. It will increase pressure in any situation and reveal possible weakness in the training and cerebral conditioning of law enforcement and hired security present. The result, lack of proper restraint, measurable destruction and harm to innocent bystanders and campaign fodder for totally insufficient local administration and blaming other the heretofore elected officials in charge of the pertinent location.

Now let's consider the obverse of this coin. The increase in automatic accusations against law enforcement regardless of the nature of the incident or involvement is forcing many police officers to literally avoid certain prescribed functions in fear of being unjustly accused, charged and possibly invalidly prosecuted for unwarranted actions or not performing their assigned duties fully within the scope of existing police policy. It is here the political forces become cowardly amenable to the raucous voice of the unwarranted activist challenges. This further diminishes the effectiveness of the individual officer and his or her immediate supervisor. All becoming mere pawns on the ever present local and national political chessboard.

The instigators of these crowd eruption are either trained or paid employees of the particular group wanting such turmoil or that small cadre of younger disenchanted individuals who too often consider their own inability to be an effective part of society or any acceptable or traditional cause. Now what of the majority of the crowd, those who honestly believe their efforts are part of the noble heritage gained in that part of the First Amendment; "or the right of the people peaceably to assemble, and to petition the Government for redress of grievances." Normally this is the basic premise for most protests. It is however, lamentable that many of the younger members of such crowds may not have rationally reviewed the particular event or cause or desired change. They either accept the media's pronouncement and that of synthetic experts without they, themselves, taking the time to look closely into the details of what they are emotionally urged to protest. Or their need to conduct their own review of the situation is overtaken by the influence of fellow advocates, too often also unequipped to handle the magnitude of their actions.

The nobility of many such protests is laudable but often wasted when the opportunity to materially voice their opinion and demands for change comes each national, state or local Election Day. The vote has been extended to 18 year olds. Some have claimed even the youthful 16 year old should have that right. That proposal scares me. Having a new cadre of potential voters who find the barely intelligible grunting of a Justin Bieber or the histrionic rantings of their favorite rapper, screaming obscenities about subjects they have little knowledge or understanding, as their conduit as to who should lead our country or their local urban area. Nevertheless, recent voting records reflect the dismal turnout of the 18 to 24 year olds, and surprisingly among those in the realm of the collegiate age group.

To achieve this desired change, regardless of the nature of the cause, to halt, to review, to change in whatever manner, it is the elected officials who have the only real power to effect change. To pursue systems and processes that would measurably correct deficiencies in such things as public security, law enforcement procedure, social welfare and care and maintenance of the highest level of human rights for all who may have or will enter this country. Without the vote, the mechanism of governance remains in the hands of the current operators. If the shoveling of the dirt is not sufficient, don't destroy the shovel, change the person handling the shovel.

What I've viewed on the television screen those months of 2020, surmount the lofty aims of a majority of the protestors, which was honoring the memory of those victims who have suffered the inexcusable indignities and improper actions of certain members of law enforcement. These uncontrolled and disastrous crowd eruptions have demeaned both the memory of these victims and the causes for which the protests were arranged. This is not to disparage the normal protest attendee. The initial attendees have taken their personal time and depending on location and distance, possibly expended a fair amount of effort to forthright present their support for or opposition to some measure or conduct by other individuals or groups. They are the promise and intent of that part of the First Amendment to assure that watchfulness and voiced opinion are never diminished or prohibited as enumerated in its final phrase ". . . and to petition the Government for redress of grievances."

It is the insidious nature of the agitators or detritus of society that attempt to enclose themselves in the envelope of a protesting group in order to create a false impression of the crowds' true intent and to endanger those others who attend. Remembering Rudyard Kipling's caution when he wrote in the early Twentieth Century, "That we may walk unbowed by fear or favor of the crowd." Much of the purposeful devastation at protests can be reduced to a degree but only by either forceful and sufficient security forces or the willingness of the honorable members of the protest to deny the core group the wherewithal to conduct their planned assault. But too often that merely enflames the more liberal and progressive segment of any such event to immediately claim their rights involved in the protest's entirety should be fully immune from any heavier security enforcement. And their actions should be immune from repercussion or criticism.

Yes, I've seen those faces and their maleficent associates too many times, at too many large events and when good people gather to be entertained, educated, or at times, when necessary, to voice their own calls for remorse or resolution. As long as there exists in society the natural urge to gather for whatever purpose, those particular faces of willful discontent will still be present. Still, there will remain that virulent contamination that I fear will never be eliminated. To diminish this type of exaggerated public tragedies, the organizations, their funding sources and any political sufferance must be uncovered. Without a diligent approach to this revelation of the suspected but unknown, the mantra, "burn baby, burn" may become a national slogan among those groups intending to exert their opinion in any manner – regardless of the results.

Chapter 5

A Revered Document Often Abused

Since the cacophony of voices and cries of constitutional protection is the equivalency of total immunity from unfavorable consequences, this writer feels this might be an appropriate time to review the most misquoted document in the history of our nation. The immediate response by those being accused, or simply questioned as to their involvement or knowledge of any matter not normally considered above suspicion as to intent or result. A response by arresting, questioning or interrogating police officers or other law enforcement agents.

To begin this portion of this essay, here is my belief regarding the United States Constitution. It is the covenant of free men that structures our governance. It is the compact that fulfills through its articles of conformation, dictates those basic rules, permissions, prohibitions and penalties that provides the ever growing body of law and its ancillary statutes. We have laws that are the cohesive substance needed to bind ever tenuously this loose fabric of society. The succinctly evidence the basic concept of the legal system and the multitude of resources, requirements and prohibitions which must be understood

"The value of law lies not in the happiness it creates, but rather the misery and suffering it prevents," Justice Lord William L. Markby, Calcutta, India High Court, 1868 "Elements of Law" Others have later ostensibly spoke to the same maxim, that if we forget the law we give our past no meaning, our future no hope and today becomes mired in self-doubt and indecision. The law and its structure of personal rights and human liberty is our gift to our children at a price they can never repay.

The media's fervor to pursue indiscretions of others and their declaration of higher moralistic standards to be adhered to by society, disguises and shields from any public scrutiny their own human frailty. Thus our self-appointed judges of both print and broadcast mediums are themselves vicars of a religious of hypocrisy. They too often espouse a display of public moralizing which accomplishes little more than to stir the dust and cloud the truth. Man has one capacity not endowed to other organisms; that of the power to reason. For only in the mind of man can an idea be conceived, given substance and born unto eventual reality. Thomas Jefferson spoke of seeking public office and said, at that moment the corruption begins. Furthermore he talked that when man assumes a public trust he should consider himself as public property, a position also needing the acquiescence of the judicial.

The Constitution is not a criminal code, it is a theory of government and is not to be read in favor of anybody as once voiced by Supreme Court Justice

David J. Brewer. Criticism in recent years has been thrust at particularly the High Court contending their various decisions have at times reflected in certain decisions as restating the subject law or legislation in a newly interpreted form. Thus the question, is the judiciary acting in a legislative role which would be in clear violation of the separation of powers and enumerated in the US Constitution? An anonymous comment can be found forwarding that "The judiciary cannot be a surrogate for public opinion or emotion." If it becomes the willing compatriot of the Congress or the silent partner to the Executive it loses the impartiality desired and required by the Founding Fathers in order to lessen the profligate abuse suffered by those governments and empires gone before. Regrettably a remark by Justice Charles Evans Hughes would give some fuel for their criticism when he said, "The constitution is what the judges say it is."

We look to the Supreme Court and a majority of its lower level judicial sites for the truth in the application of the law, but we need to realize truth is the human interpretation of fact and the constant vacillation by our political and media reveals the most evident the flaw in our specie. When the power is excessively attempted without legal purpose against the courts we begin the ultimate deterioration of the basic rights given to and enjoyed by the citizenry. This is why such actions by either the legislature or the White House must be constantly monitored to avoid this disrepair of our government. And in equal sense why the High Court must continually assess its role as a judge and not arbiter or social solace provider to the masses. Thus we look to the fabled Bill of Rights as the asserted guarantor of our freedoms as being explicit in that document.

Of all the amendments and attending phraseology of the Constitution, it is the First Amendment that identifies and stipulates those basic freedoms for which the American Revolution was fought and the eventual following wars were waged, regardless of the varying opinions as to their being improper or imprecise in meaning or worth. The First Amendment protects words that persuade, not words to incite. Although so simply stated by its writers, there exists a continuing review of these rights that is constantly being clarified, interpreted or challenged.

Yet strictures issued by the court can create hypothetical statements; veiled threats to reconstitute the primary format of that document when appearing to hear the voice of contemporary society. In doing so there arises the specter of self-induced righteousness. Regardless of the intended nobility of such an action, such position is not within the oath of any judge or magistrate.

The elasticity of the First Amendment is constantly being tested. It cannot however, immune ones involvement in the actual commission of a crime or the proven contribution to a conspiracy or attempt to supersede its primary purpose. Still "Free speech is not so absolute or irrational a conception so as to paralyze the other freedoms of the Bill of Rights," as posed by Justice Hugo Black in rendering a minority opinion relative to a case regarding the parameters of the First Amendment.

The Constitution has weathered many assaults upon the intent of its writers and its correctness by those who would contend their interpretation is the truest image as envisioned as fulfilling the needs and desires of the common man they so ardently proclaim they represent. It is critical for any nation's survival that man has no greater voice than the laws that govern his existence. It must be understood that what man desires in clarification of its right and the law is structured to require, the legislators will too often confuse and attorneys will convolute to meet the need of their clients. Wisdom is that which we recognize as correct only after the original intent of the act. The law is the bastard child of justice which still holds the sword of vigilance. Regardless of the extent of accusations brought against anyone, Justice Oliver Wendell Holmes wrote, "The law should be stable but never stand still," which however, does not give the judiciary free reign to interpret in light of current social demand or to curry favor with the masses.

Additionally, it is the most utilized amendment by those demanding their specific rights and freedom to pursue activities which others might feel are inopportune not desired. It is that last phrase referred to earlier, concerning ". . . right of the people to peaceably to assemble . . ." that we direct attention regarding the primary substance of this paper, the protest movement and its ancillary conditions and possible adversarial results. When that final phrase is dissected word for word we see "peaceable" and then "redress for grievances." It is difficult to remember those words and equate them with scenes of burning buildings or mobs of people breaking through plate glass fronts to stores and later seen fleeing with armloads of materials, often expensive clothes or electronics.

The local police or other security may at time appear either immobile or seemingly unable to respond. But today's liberal demands for group constitutional rights and the failure of local administration to support their police departments leaves little room or decision in such matters. To move on the fire bombers and looters is to have a massively increased security force present. Or to use drastic measures to either forestall or apprehend the malefactors at the site will immediately bring cries from protestors and political figures alike accusing said security forces of misconduct and possible legal consequences.

If either measure is used the instant claim of police brutality and excessive force would be shouted. The media present would devote total coverage on any such actions or claims by those affected. Later adjudication would be first targeted on the claimed police abuse of their power and the potential harm to the assured rights of all the protestors. A conundrum mixed within a quandary with little result except as the deterioration of the relationship between the public and law enforcement. A common problem for the police when one is expected to defend against a charging beast while carrying only a simple willow switch. And within this plethora of chants and invectives so much a part of the protest dialogue reference is always the singular right granted them in the Constitution, ". . . or the right of the people to peaceably assemble . . ." Sadly the expression "peaceably assemble." with no attendant mandate for allowing violence seems to have been forgotten.

There is a maxim that you can't make a garment of legal justification without at least a shred of the cloth of the Constitution. The basis of law is its direct association to an acceptable degree with both the language of that document and the primary premise of its writers. As the law is that adhesive that melds the framework of our social and economic structure, without it we become only an assembly of disjointed personal and political agendas. We need now to direct our attention to those very laws whose interpretation and implementation first generated by those permissions and prohibitions that re prescribed or referred to in the Constitution. "People crushed by laws have no hope but to gain power. If the law is their enemy they will become enemies of the law," was purported by Edmund Burke. The law is the fabric of man's dream to live forever and without the fear of no greater master than he himself has imagined.

As to the actual laws referred to in the rights listed in the First Amendment and their application regarding the multitude of potential offenses that can and too often does occur as the type of aggravated protest scenes we've experienced lately are more likely to be viewed as protecting the offender. Disregarding the innocent business firm burned out of service, possibly never to return, little has been publicly mentioned and as to compensation, the resources to reopen, little has been offered by the local administration.

Too often it has been viewed literally as inconsequential by the media, as strictly another example of exemption from fault under the cloak of the First Amendment. That same part of the constitution they will quickly use to protect any criticism of their coverage of the protest itself. We demand defined systems for education, technical training, the practice of law and medicine before being accepted in the professional ranks. But where is the combined assessment of personal and group fault and the legal basis for compensating those so injured and economically devastated by protests such as we have witnessed for more than four months. Yet, when defending a protest participant faced with misdemeanor or felony charges and possible financial penalty, voila! There appears that inevitable reference to the First Amendment, the supposed constitutional get out of jail card.

Of course journalists normally don't face any type of accusations for their actions or lack thereof other than the complaints arising from distortion of detail and inference of facts that may or may not be corroborated. Yet journalists are really lawyers at heart and both suffer from a tedious obsession with fact. The journalist feigns objectivity in dealing with information discovered while the lawyer feigns outrage when such information is used as evidence. A few attorneys when dealing with protest participants arrests and accusations begin to believe they are the voice of the law and not merely the extension of sufficient legal knowledge and experience to provide the client with fair representation before the bar of justice.

It must first understood that the union initially intended by the Constitution was formed from a disparate group of concepts, ideologies, cultural definitions and personal agendas. The gathering of those providing prosed language, the actual writers of the eventual document and those who would debate rigorously regarding the multitude possible inclusions, in that time, the late 18th Century, was not comprised of average individuals but persons of far higher institutionalized education than enjoyed by most of the then population. Furthermore they were consider leaders or individuals of stature in their particular home areas. In many instances, erudite and articulate in expressing themselves and supported by their yet to be formulated constituency to be the selected spokespersons for interest in and desire for what became the United States Constitution.

This particular dialogue will deal with that document as it refers in part or specifically to the eventual tripartite form of governing structure that was effected. We will cover the element of control of poser, the supremacy of each body in certain functional responsibilities and the continuing question of what changes, alterations and/or interpretation is needed to bring this revered instrument into compliance with the social, economic, racial and political ideologies most currently dominant.

Pertinent will be the power of the executive branch and the thin line between the rights given to administer and the laws governing same. The legislative branch and the degree to which they attempt or actually have the lawfully mandated functions prescribed in the constitution. Finally, the Supreme Court and the question of supremacy in determining the scope of authority allowed the other branches and the determining factor in matters of policy, legislative extension and the direction or expansion of the constitution. The assertions by some groups to be allowed a semblance of interference into the sole authority of the legislative branch to propose, prepare and initial laws, statutes and regulations that affect the lives of the general public cannot be allowed unless defined by a legally proposed constitutional amendment.

This essay cannot plumb the full depths of academic consideration or potential effects of drastically change or reevaluation of the purpose and intent of this document. To form a good and effective Constitution, you must assure the complete involvement of the liberty of the individual coupled with a strong and government. If either are too dominant or too weakened in its association with the other, failure to achieve and eventual dissolution by force will occur. Today's decried social evils are the results of ignorance of the administration of a free government and the neglect of the natural rights of man. We should always note that when we inaugurate or appoint any official, they swear to preserve, protect and defend the Constitution and not the government of any particular group or belief. It is this salient point that too often distorts the image of any one in elected or appointed authority.

It is believed the framers of the original constitution did not foresee the creation and development of political parties as is now being experienced and in those early days possibly little considered they would be of little import as referred to implementation of the constitution. They made no provision for their participation or involvement in the prohibitions and permissions other than as reflected therein. The entirety of the document is awash with the original belief by its writers that imperfect men should not be expected to produce a thoroughly clear and non-debatable document. That change and interpretation would follow and with that thought, an inevitable amendment process.

The tripartite form of government, its three distinct branches, Executive, Legislative and Judicial remains the structure we currently employ. The presidency, the chief executive of the nation is the positional flashpoint since the beginning of the nation. It is the one individual selected, along with a vice presidential associate, as the leader of the country, the singular image to many throughout the world. As a result it becomes the target of criticism, debate, and contestation during its administration and attempts to remove either by impeachment of forced acquiescence to the demands of the opposing political party. It is this conflict of wills and demands for control that has caused the plethora of constitutionally based litigations and eventual static resistance by one or the other.

We know that evolution proceeds, whether within species or cultural or societal groupings it is quite difficult to evolve as a structural change in a Constitution or charter or even a covenant however sincere the desire and need to emerge new forms or interpretations. Thomas Jefferson and Alexander Hamilton, early on argued the question of expansion or extension of either prohibitions or permissions as originally stated in the Constitution. Hamilton favored interpretation in the language of the specific area of contention. Jefferson insisted such change had to be by amendment when he wrote in 1803, "Let us go on perfecting the Constitution by adding by way of amendment, those forms which time and trial show are still wanting." A more favored alternative in extending or restating certain aspects of the Constitution was found in the amendment requirements, allowing a degree of elasticity without protecting the security of what was being proposed until the proper process was implemented. This was needed as the interpretation of that document had become a tool to politicize the process and interpretation was separated more and more from the literal meaning of the Constitution's language.

As the framers of the original constitution did not foresee the creation and development of political parties as thus made no provision for their participation or involvement in the administration of the prohibitions and permissions allowed therein. When this developed, the immediate result was the interpretation of contested portions of the constitution leading to congressional action, potential denial by the executive branch and ultimately the entire matter becoming the property of the court's domain. The one method to discourage constant amendment requests or demands was by ignoring such innovative or altering insertions attempts until they were legally challenged. It then became the right of the Supreme Court to either expand the interpretation of certain Constitutional language or to fill in those blank spaces they feel would answer the initial inquiry.

To those intent on speedier changes or interpretative alteration of parts of the Constitution, their ability to take full control of any such revisions or redirection of the prohibitions and permissions contained therein without legal restraint or conditions, it could be strongly contended that the constitution no longer belonged to the people – and the people alone without inappropriate interference by others, whether in authoritative or activist position.

What is noticeable about the system and method of administration adopted in the initial Constitutional format is that the legislature branch was permitted to initiate and/or ratify so many aspects directing the nature of the government's approach to policy, law, financial regulation and social inclusion, particularly in the form of basically altering the actual language of the original constitution. In its original form, the executive and judicial branches appeared to have been excluded. That to propose, prepare and present matters that could be part of any constitutional convention was exclusively that of the legislature. Thus making any proposed amendment outside this controlled format impossible. Fortunately that was altered in the early days of the Constitution's formation.

Chapter 6

When the Black Robes Become Tattered

It should be noted that as this essay was being edited, the report of the death at age 87 of Supreme Court Associate Justice, Ruth Bader Ginsburg shocked the nation. Although this writer and others may not have always agreed with her rulings and particular interpretations of constitutional issues, her laudable record of the high court will be difficult for any new member to ever achieve. She was a national icon in her staunch defense and active effort for the continuing growth of women's rights and the fair application of the law to both they and the minority classes. Confirmed by then President Bill Clinton in 1993, she was a tireless student of the law and fervent advocate for the poor. Her rise through the legal ranks itself was a credit to her personal and professional strength of purpose. The effect of her loss from the bench and the political implications regarding the ability or wisdom of attempting to nominate and confirm a replacement during this emotionally tense pre and post-election period is a subject better left to those with far more expertise and experience in such sensitive matters. The final resolution may easily change the character of the United States Supreme court for the next decade or more.

Over the years the Supreme Court has demonstrated time and time again its inability to maintain a fully objective review as they cannot divorce themselves, individually or as a group from any inherent bias. That its prejudices and preset ideological considerations have been and will always be present, however latent at times or secured in the language used in rendering decisions. Their claim that such interpretations are mandatory and in no way reflect bias but rather a totally subjective review has its self been criticized by those demanding less political sufferance on the part of the courts at all levels.

It must be emphasized that the word 'interpretation' does not appear anywhere in the Constitution. However, since the Court, as early as Marbury vs. Madison was rendered, when invented by that same Court, it has remained subject to the whims or wills of the nine justices, however disjointed they may be on any particular matter brought before them. To the students of the Constitution it was understood that the document might be altered in some minute fashion as cases were decided. But since interpretation was not part of the language and that substantive change could could come only from amendments. The framers of the Constitution gave the Court only the powers to adjudicate "all cases in law and equity arising under the Constitution, the laws of the United States and treaties made under the authority granted the other branches."

Regrettably, it is rarely taught or emphasized that only two amendments of the entire history of our Constitution have measurably affected the structure of our government. The first referenced the election of Senators and the other, limiting presidents to serving of no more than two terms. The First Amendment states "The Congress shall make no law . . ." and the rest refers to concurrent prohibitions. The Supreme Court has no perceivable instructions or permissions to involve themselves in the formulating new recitations of the law or 'interpretations', their primary claim to authority is 'jurisdiction', the ability to assume a judicial review as countenanced within the present constitutional language. It has been espoused the Congress may have exceeded its original intent when they passed and revised laws establishing the operation of the judiciary, both at the national and later sub-level or lesser courts. The acts and statutory guidance went beyond the clause of the Constitution creating and empowering the judiciary other than constituting courts inferior to the Supreme Court as referred to in Art. 1, Sect. 8.

To many, the Court appears to have an immunity to rebuke of any nature, its growing role of supremacy in the performance of its legal review seeming to protect it from any material changes. As the original Founding Fathers and framers of the Constitution were attorneys, today that specific occupational background is even more pronounced. As if every law degree holding legislator may subliminally feel they are their own Supreme Court with all its rights and privileges. The entirety of the Constitution is awash with the original belief by its writers that imperfect men should not be expected to produce a thoroughly clear and non-debatable document. That change and varied interpretation would follow and with that thought, the need for the amendment process.

Andrew Hamilton expressed the opinion that he viewed the Supreme Court's judges themselves as the weakest aspect of that branch. This arose from the decision that both the President and Congress would have the power to form and shape the structure of the presiding justices. The President to appoint but subject to approval of the Senate. Additionally the Congress could designate inferior courts and determine pertinent jurisdiction. It was felt the complete independence of the courts was critical considering the limitation of expression in many of the clauses of the Articles and the Amendments themselves.

With the increasing intrusion of the political factor in selecting and approving the lower court membership, the question of required impartiality has become moot. Although interpretation of the laws is the specific province of the courts, there arises the distinct feeling that many judges do not consider the Constitution as law. Making judicial supremacy in all its functions as only constitutional supremacy and immune to any type of structural or conceptual interference. The question remains, will opponents of the present constitutional amendment requirement develop any way to revise the law without amending it?

The constitution can appear ambiguous regarding such use or demand for extraordinary powers. However, it has to be thought that such a myriad of crises might not be in the future of the new and as yet thoroughly developed governing structure. It was agreed early in our nation's formation that the new government would face needs or increased responsibilities and that the Constitution should not stand in in the way. That it must be flexible in order to meet and deal with these expected new responsibilities. Thus came the axiom deemed paramount in considering future actions by both branches that anything not prohibited is permitted. The position and influence of the Congress within the prohibitions and permissions of the constitution are constantly questioned. It was insisted that constitutional questions must require constitutional resolution and solution. That to allow the Congress to become the arbiter's of interpretation and administration of that document's critical allowances and prohibitions would be to politicize what was to be the people's voice.

The issue of states' rights has long been contested, some saying it was the direct cause of the Civil War and remains a divisive issue in many legislative controversies. Article V was initially felt to resolve the matter when it stated that "no state, without its consent, shall be deprived of its equal suffrage in the Senate. This is where the equality of representation for all states, then and added, sits a limitation to single party control of all legislative matters. It further was to set limits the the amendment process.

Within the legislative process the repeated moves of each branch of government when resisted or claimed without power to effect desired actions, is too often defended by those who consider it merely a manner of reaching an acceptable balance. Yet, the rise of political interplay and lack of compromise plus voting control has diminished that claim to mere verbal jousting. It becomes a constant struggle to determine the limits of power expressed by one branch or another and such systematic combat flows downward into the many subordinate agencies and commissions mandated to execute and implement the wishes of Congress and/or the executive branch.

In the arena of exercised power the effort to assume formerly unquestioned control is a most dangerous activity during times of war and/or potential insurrection. The immediate provision of extraordinary power, particularly to the executive branch is then ameliorated by succeeding demands and actions as such warfare continues and creates increased political division and/or public disorder. It has occurred numerous times, with Andrew Johnson after Lincoln's assassination, Franklin Roosevelt at the outset of WW II and continued with Kennedy and Truman, Johnson and Nixon as involved the Korean War and the Vietnam crisis.

The members of both the high and lower courts may disagree often but have always held to one rule of operation that they keep to themselves the power to determine when and where these emergency conditions exists. Particularly when they feel one branch or the other have exceeded their powers as referred to in the Constitution or as they interpret that emergency. Article 1, Section 8 of the constitution gives Congress the right "to make all laws which shall be necessary and proper for carrying into execution the foregoing powers and all other powers vested by this constitution n in the government of the united States, or in any department or officer thereof." It is this extremely broad language that has created the maelstrom of conflict between the executive and legislative branch and permeated the lowest level of operating and regulatory agencies.

The Supreme Court opposed the attempt by the then Congress to limit the jurisdiction of the courts as being in violation of the tripartite concept of the original constitutional format. It was this decision that began the ascendency of the national government in any disputes with any of the states. Later it became standard preclusion that the powers explicit to the government was exclusive. The states were not to be allowed to interfere with any agency of the government through the machinery of taxation. It was argued in the early days of our nation that the authority of the national government came directly from the people and not from the states as individual entities. This was the beginning the continuing tests for determining the position of implied powers within the language of the constitution

Chief Justice John Marshall early on emphasized the supremacy clause, particularly in those litigations forwarded by the states in their demand to be allowed taxation rights over agencies of the government. Marshall's salient view was that the people did not design their government to be subservient to the states. Again, placement of the Supreme Court as the final resolution with no adversarial recourse permitted.

As initially argued in reference to a highly contested proposal for a national bank in the late 18th Century, the controversy later became the 10th amendment and a prominent statement encompassed in the amendment's language, "The powers not delegated to the United States by the Constitution, nor prohibited by it to the states are reserved the states respectively." Simply put, 10th Amendment restricts the powers of the government except as specifically delegated to them or to the obverse prohibited to the states, all other powers are reserved to the states or to the agencies and officials of those states.

When one attempts to understand whether the terms strict or loose construction of the constitution, it becomes a question, which is the controlling factor. As a result, it is felt this is the reason the court has become the sole administrator and decider as to any expansion of both intent and interpretation of the constitution itself. However, there are those who feel that in last few decades the constitution is just a product of the Supreme Court's interpretation coupled with any bias or predetermination that may exist? Thus, the reading of the document becomes more ambiguous with every court presentation. To those who don't wish to see any measurable change in the impact of the constitution, it is their view that such involvement by the court makes what is ostensibly an imprecise document, acceptable at a minimum when palatable to the majority of the court.

One of the most defining element of the national legislative process, filtering down even into local administration, is the fact that when power has substantive control it becomes a monopoly and as often proven, monopolies seldom relinquish their power. This is often evidenced by the inaction of legislative pursuit of critical issues, crippled by the primary intent to amass and maintain power without defining potentially controversial positions. Yet to the anarchist, the avid revolutionary, the rabid extremist, this demand for abdication of power in a need or desire for compromise is unacceptable and that control can only be accomplished through violent seizure and physical assault of the entity holding the power.

As expressed in the constitution, the ability of the legislature to enact laws, administer the implementation of individuals rights and to execute taxing is derived from the will of the people It is a positive and voluntary act by the electorate and cannot be assumed by any governmental branch or agency without express permission of legislature, approval by the executive and countenanced by the high court. Simply, the legislature, at any level, cannot transfer their authority and responsibility to make laws and place it in the operational hands of others.

It has been said that the constitution cannot accomplish what is impossible or impracticable except through the mandated amendment process. With the division of thought regarding the court's seeming intent to revise through interpretation, alteration or addition of actual laws, permissions and prohibitions spoken of in the constitution. An action also becoming more apparent in the lower courts. Is it possible that the safeguards of the intent and integrity of the rights encompassed in the Constitution are being diminished by the constant compromises that serve only those proposing and opposing measures they are willing to accept with suitable benefit to both political parties contending and not the people as a whole?

There remains a danger in radically disturbing the substance of the original constitutional intent by allowing too excessive an influence by public passions. The amendments formulated since the first ten were adopted have regrettably been formulated and accepted without too much inspection as to the effect on the document as a whole. The web of government involvement touches every political, social, economic and foreign policy aspect of daily life in the United States. There is the constant theme that the constitutional language and its former intent have deteriorated over the years. That advancing social norms and the pressure of a technology that allows greater public input requires change in a number of the basic tenets of both the constitution itself and its coupled Bill of Rights and amendments. The constitution mandates a method and subsequent statutes detail systems for such changes or rephrasing. It requires a bevy of supporters and numerous state government approvals before a substantive alterations can even be brought to vote by both the legislatures and the public itself in one form or another.

Many questions and unresolved issues still face both the responsibility of the legislature, which affects the position of the executive branch and seemingly permits even greater influence of the courts however, dubious. As to the issue of "extraordinary powers" discussed earlier, critics contend there too often has been the assumption of that right be unquestioned during war or martial law. It has been argued for elimination of such powers to minimize future instances of increased involvement by government through intervention not specifically allowed by congressional approval. That basically the question arises as to the position and influence of the Congress within the prohibitions and permissions of the constitution. The advocates of strict constructionism insist that all constitutional questions must require constitutional resolution and solution. It is here the position of the Supreme Court gains the greatest and most intense scrutiny.

With the advent of political partisanship within the legislative process came the axiom regarding all future actions that what is not prohibited is permitted. That the court's right was ostensibly to say what the constitution meant, in reality the ultimate level of decision making. From that point in our nation's history it was felt by most that such power was exclusive to the high court. It should be emphasized here that the word "interpretation" does not appear anywhere in the constitution.

It is rarely taught or emphasized that only two amendments of the entire history of the constitution have actually affected to any degree the structure of our government; the 17th Amendment concerning the election of Senators and the 22nd Amendment limiting president's to serving no more than two terms. All the rest clarify or eliminate previous constitutional prohibitions or allow actions previously either disregarded or insufficient in substance and implementation. The writers of the constitution gave the newly proposed court only the powers to adjudicate "all cases in law and equity arising under the constitution, the laws of the United States and treaties made under the authority granted other branches." Still the cry arises that the courts are interfering in the legally endowed legislative process and the governing powers applicable to the executive branch. An opinion too often engendered by the type and nature of questioning of Supreme Court nominees and the questioned loyalties of lower court justices. The function of the Supreme Court is to interpret the Constitution as it is presently written, not as the members may want to see it written.

There remains an inherent danger in radically disturbing the substance of the original constitutional intent by allowing too excessive an influence on the amendment process by the intensity of public passion. The original ten amendments were formulated, regrettably by possibly too little time to resolve each of the potential issues contained therein. But since the web of government, its extensive and growing outreach touches and affects every aspect of daily life in its social, economic, political and foreign policy actions, it is suspected that integrity of the rights guaranteed by that same constitution are the possible victims in any headlong dash to change without purpose and eventual effect.

Chapter 7

Come Aboard the Ship of Fools

We are now at that point where we can discuss a targeted majority of the deserved criticism for our continuing descent into the abyss of national self-destruction, unless major changes occur. Ladies and gentlemen, our Congress is next. 535 members who form a cornucopia of legislative incontinence. We have faced no less than four major disease epidemics that have ravaged millions over the past century. Influenza or the `flu' which caused millions of deaths and in recent years still a deadly visitor when it rises to epidemic level. Ebola that has decimated parts of the population in numerous African nations. The deadly SARS virus which fortunately has been contained to a degree but still presents an ever present threat. And now, the outbreak of what is termed coronavirus or Covid-19, already infecting millions and caused thousands of deaths.

First announced in southern China where it seemed to originate, it now affects countries throughout the world with the United States suffering in large numbers. Hopefully its source can soon be determined and medical resources and proven vaccines developed to combat its long range debilitating and deadly effect on our economic, social and governmental functioning. Trump has been castigated for what his opponents declare was his late issuance of warnings. The WHO, World Health Organization, knew of the threat months earlier but failed to inform anyone of importance – at least importance or influence to their status. But then again, they, like so many other ostensibly global research organizations, appear to never have any connective response to similar entities elsewhere other than their own desire to retain a posture and reclusiveness they neither were granted nor will relinquish.

However, there is another virulent, pervasive and little recognized virus here in our country that creates socio-economic, political and governance maladies. It is political aspiration. An infectious entry into the human psyche that engenders personality and emotional changes in the normal function of the rational mind and action. It begins as an imagined idea that one can actually be a dominant force for change in what is considered by the individual as a world disaffected by the perils of corruption, or excessive control or inadequate equality within his or her personal domain. To achieve this desired representative posture, one must garner the support of colleagues, associates or parties interested in the use of the individual's rising prominence to enhance their own personal agenda or specific objectives. When eventually enclosed within this bubble of rising popularity and acceptance as a viable political candidate, regardless the office or position, the individual begins the direct effort to assure added resources, both fiscal and supportive. Once the goal of elective office success has been achieved, the latent virus of ambition and desired notice begins to spread into the natural patterns of logical consideration, rational assumption and the need to recognize when compromise can and often does further the individual's sincerely held goals or intents.

Regardless how exhilarating the initial access to the House of Representatives or the Senate by the victor upon their first election victory, there will very soon arrive the disheartening facts of life within the political enclosure. As to being a freshman legislator, possibly from a relatively indistinct and little recognized district even in one's home state, the odyssey from unfamiliarity to anonymity begins. The new delegate will soon learn of the many former broom closets available in the various office buildings when first measuring the limited dimensions of his or her first office suite. To many, the description will be more architectural than factual. From there it is the selection of staff, most often at least one to three from the home state district. The shock on the faces of these new acolytes at the altar of the chosen members of Congress, will appear the moment they realize the housing conundrum.

Not to forget limitations in nearby locations, available space available and the prices for what in their home area would be considered, diplomatically phrased, as obscene. Of course a slight benefit is present to the new staff member. They are not required to maintain a legal residence back home as will their new congressional employer. With increasing costs for every staple of life and the supposed taxpayer obstinacy in moving for more reasonable legislative salaries, I am reminded by an old clique that reflects why many cannot or will not take on such a challenge: If you pay peanuts you get monkeys, monkeys are all you will get.

With those economic onslaughts finally recognized as the life's vicissitudes they will be subjected to, it is now the time for the new legislator to position him or herself in the temple of synodical effort. Prime committee assignments are the medallions necessary to gain both availability to the actual law making process and of course, a noted presence to draw the media interest. It is only in the glare of the TV camera light or the recorded statements for the endless mélange of news reporters that the congress habitué has any opportunity to let the folks back home how wise they were in his or her selection.

Now firmly implanted in his or her new persona, that of the "Honorable Representative of his or her district located in his or her home state, there begins the waiting component of the novice legislator's new life. There are approximately on hundred standing committees in the House of Representatives and seventeen or so in the Senate, not to forget the ten or so select committees or seventy or more seventy sub-committees in the Senate structure. This is the confusing myriad of individual assignments and potential opportunities. But as the the new legislator will soon discover, it is the ever present shadow of the special interest activist and lobbyists that often hold the upper hand.

It will soon be clear to the honorable representative that below this ostensibly highest level of legislative authority and policy creation, will be found the actual messengers of the mandates forthcoming from the House chamber where the party hierarchy dwells. They are the ones charged with the responsibility, whether appropriate or even constitutionally viable, to assign such details to those they feel can most effectively achieve the desired results. Even so, it will also be discovered that such administrators must be protected from excessive knowledge, since too much knowledge denudes them of the required cloak of immunity necessary to maintain their own self-preservation and that of their immediate superiors. It's a simple element of surviving in our nation's capital. This minimization of the entirety of any project or operation or administration is the required armor of congressional insusceptibility in the event others might begin to question the efficacy or legality of certain measures or propositions.

Most important is assuring the protection of the political framework in power. Excessive knowledge is dangerous to unexpected revelations of misinformation or implausible purposes to any new policy. The new legislator soon learns that ignorance is a cherished and vital asset to leadership, if and inevitably when disclosure of less enviable aspects of some project or questionable undertaking becomes a reality. The less the principal authority knows of the required operational or productive details, the less the chance for early revision or rejection of the initial policy decision.

Too much extraneous knowledge impairs the ability of high-ranking officials in any governmental entity to be protected if they are privy to the reality of the situation. An inconvenience which might force them to tell the truth when being required to respond at any public inquiry. This assures the strength of their impunity to criticism or retribution by external or legal forces. It is the operational details not required tasks for the power structure but a burden borne by many lower level administration staff. It is this procedural anagram the new legislator must accept, even if its full import may never be totally understood unless or until extended returns to the Halls of Congress allows both its cognizance and eventual use to preserve personal agendas and careers.

To successively achieve or implement the intents of the governing authority as originally intended by our Founding Fathers, it is imperative that one recognizes it is this created convolution of goals and personal objectives that populates inside what the media has designated the "beltway." It is a lesson that must be immediately understood or the new legislator will soon find themselves back home among their decreasing admirers and more importantly, absent financial donors. And while this confusing matrix is being dealt with, within a year of being elected, the new legislator must face another campaign effort, the need to increase vote margin and of course, the ever increasing cost of joining his or her colleagues back in Congress. As one anonymous twit observed, campaigning for reelection is much like undergoing that operation critical to your sustaining life – except again, without any form of anesthetic.

The rampant series of revelations, automatic congressional hearings and if course, the required newest books exposing something or someone all engenders the same question. What is to be to be disclosed, who is to be blamed and what is the truth? And with the seamier aspects of some of the disclosures, regardless of source, it is said that scandal always seems to have a running start while the truth is forced to crawl. Former President, Harry S. Truman once told an interviewing reporter, "I never give the public hell, I just tell the truth and they think its's hell." Fortunately for George Washington, in his time he didn't have to lie about anything since the income tax didn't exist nor did congressional hearings. When one considers that over fifty percent of the Senators have law degrees and thirty-eight percent of the House of Representatives are also attorneys, it brings to mind a comment by French poet and playwright Jean Giraudoux when he wrote, "No poet ever interpreted nature as freely as a lawyer interprets the truth."

That distinctive gold embellished insignia pin always significantly viewable on the legislator's collar, whatever his or her rank might be in the current hierarchy, to the newer members, may eventually seem to have the weight of that biblical millstone. With the image of a Representative or Senator and very often the President filling the TV screen with press briefings or automatic response to another colleagues comments and the invariable interviews one begins to wonder. A group of people who hear everything and understand nothing. Who keep the subterfuge to themselves, always nodding when acceptance by the speaker is indicated or required based on party loyalty. Regrettably, where once the individuals sent by a believing constituency solid as the statue but impervious to the inclement weather of criticism and unassailable by the storms of favoritism. Today the members of Congress have become mere legislative sponges, absorbing every possible benefit and external influence. They appear unable to resist the rot of ambition and the mold of absolute party loyalty in disregard of how such fealty might affect their constituency.

We have over the years become literally inured to the awareness that truth in its sublime and uncensored state is more often than not the unwanted guest at most legislative deliberations. It is an esoteric expression when gathered in the folds of, and governmental lexicon. It can bother, impede or challenge the political process as dictated by each party leadership. It is now become a lamentable but irrevocable fact that our media, cloaked in the vaunted protection of the First Amendment for over two hundred thirty years, has more recently declared a new, a modified mantra of their purpose. That the truth is what they present, in the form presented and in the manner that determines the worth or meaning or inference allowed in the insertion of the needed facts in every story, incident, occurrence or happening they will distribute for public consumption. Yet we recognize that although the truth is timeless to the ethical it is tiresome to the liar.

Yet, before we depart the much defined "swamp" as coined by its numerous critics, let us momentarily review the basic outline of the five hundred thirty five members. Within this supposed collegium there exists no less than three distinct strata. It is those who have been infused with the desire for greater power and position within the party structure who rise in committee and hierarchical prominence. It is they who determine both the submission and/or eventual passage and defeat of all legislation, regardless its merit or apparent need by the constituency. And as ones public persona and stature on the national scene increases, who knows, perhaps a chance to grab at the brass ring of ultimate political stardom – possibly one of those infinitesimally brief reaches for that 1600 Pennsylvania Ave. address. To the truly dedicated to becoming a power within the Washington DC beltway, it requires strength and duration of effort and the quickness to avoid the inevitable pitfalls and legislative landmines that will have been laid by the opposition. When such might occur it is the agile politician who is able to dodge the truth.

Unless one is a student of governmental systems and particularly our national legislature there are aspects of the House of Representatives that bear a closer perspective. As for the process of lawmaking we are a people contained within a labyrinth of governmental agencies, regulatory bodies and the maze of interlocking jurisdictions. The ability of the justice department to sanction either openly or surreptitiously investigations often enabled by use of the highly criticized and judicially suspect FISA courts to obtain warrants, sans any public or official disclosure. FISA is the Foreign Intelligence Surveillance Act created by the 95th Congress, Oct. 25, 1978. It allows issuance of secret warrants for the search, seizure or surveillance of individuals believed to be engaged in activities that threaten the national security of the country. Such warrants are acquired from a select group of judges sworn to secrecy and for which there is no recourse as to identification or reasoning for their actions. Thus their conduct is not open to review, notice or validation by any governing elements of any of the three branches.

This is a major threat on the basic principles of justification and transparency constantly proclaimed from the campaign trail by every candidate in recent decades. When the process of any segment of governmental administration, whether Executive or Legislative is undertaken in such a manner it breaches the oath taken by every elected or appointed official by interpreting to their personal needs the constitutional bounds of their authority. Whether such moves are born of urgent need to accomplish what is felt necessary for the good of the people or to remove or reduce review of by others and possible delay, measurable change or rejection. To be fair in apprising need and clarity in any presentation or proposal – or investigation – is a reasonable degree of transparency. When the desire is to avoid review and possible repercussions due to the unauthorized or invalidated aspect of the action it is necessary to employ subterfuge. Allowing that to become the norm initiates the beginnings of dictatorial control which is in direct contradiction and in violation of the precepts of the constitution.

We speak of bills being presented, many alterations are usually required before submission to endless review committees and finally to the floor of either chamber for final vote. With the desire to accomplish the greatest amount of personal advantage through add-ons or most often unrelated amendments. Every piece of legislation has more riddles than answers. A bill proposed by either party becomes a catchall to which the detritus of numerous personal embellishments by fellow or opposing colleagues must be attached like broken ornaments on a barren congressional Christmas tree. If passed it becomes a legally phrased crossword puzzle lacking legitimate or verifiable answers in order to fill in the spaces. It resembles a dense patina of indefinable language and true intent gathered within its wordage.

In the beehive of Congressional bureaucracy, those who recognize the mountainous heights required to attain any station near the top become the worker bees, serving every legislative vote needs of the establishment in power. They need to continue their presence as it provides particular perks normally unavailable in private enterprise. It furthermore enhances their heretofore unknown existence with a congressional appellation of Representative or Senator. A steady income, the necessary funding by resolute supporters each two or six years. Never to be forgotten, the monetary opportunities that always travel in tandem along the route with anyone who is is part of the highest level of national administration, the United States Congress.

For the indistinguishable first timer, specifically in the House, there is the inevitable frustration with the inability to be heard or to pursue those worthwhile and personally considered noble endeavors so earnestly promised on the initial campaign trail. Campaign funding is limited, the expense of dual lodging sustenance increasingly difficult and the when eventually the understanding that there is no substantive position for them in the power structure system that exists and has for two centuries plus, reality will appear at the door of his office. It is then home, accompanied by the frustration of little if any accomplishment and in part relieved they have been able to wade out of the brackish, muck filled bottom of that same swamp. Ambition is the cancer that begins the decimation of an individual's ethical fiber when he or she deigns to cross the Potomac and join the inhabitants of the political jungle. Yet to most of them, even worse is possible anonymity.

We have become addicted to demanding charisma from our leaders, a group selected from a large group of people, most of whom have or would initially refuse political entre but as children must have desired to run away to the circus. That feeling never completely disappears. It becomes another dream, to traipse the halls of Congress in clear view of the reporters, television cameras, microphones and the few visitors who might waste their time seeking the images of of the media created idols or dolts. It is, as Shakespeare so aptly described in his play, "As You Like It," when he wrote, "All the worlds a stage. And all the men and women merely players. They have their exits and entrances." That is the reality of survival within the fabled `Beltway' all contenders to power and position must accept.

If ever any of these aspiring champions of the people, valiant comforter of the oppressed and seekers of the truth, while on their campaign trail would ever read this section of my book, I'd suggest they heed the following bit of advice; Regardless of what has been studied in Harvard, achieved in law school or acquired through local popular acclaim or what your name is, In the bowels of the gastrointestinal upset referred to as Washington, DC, you have to know what the game is. And also, that the game is rigged and will always remain in that format unless major changes are made in the elected leadership. That reformation is only in the hands of the voter and not those who would resort to violence to create their version of what should be and in their limited understanding, isn't.

Chapter 8

Selling Words as Truth

Decades ago, while in college, I read that three factors allowed mankind to elevate themselves from the primitive Neanderthals and Cro-Magnons; the discovery of fire, development of the wheel and the evolution of organized and intelligible language. After mileniums of human conversation it now appears that method of contact, one with another has in today's accelerated technology, becomes more the movement of digital signals and indecipherable numeric babble. Still, there remains an uncontrolled addiction to expressing opinion, whether solicited or ignored and most often without pre thought. But perhaps we can debate that subject later. Inasmuch as I have undoubtedly and overtly insulted the memories of past residents in the pantheon of legislative giants inside the government and possibly considered as having cast aspersions on the present membership, it is now time to move on. So on to a part of our social disillusionment becoming more evident to the general public in recent years.

This will be a subject that had in its infancy the power of the primary tool which could affect the machinery of governance to convince, revise, propagate or eliminate legislation. Thus, either bolstering or terminating the careers of political, entertainment, sports and even social figures. That feared instrument was the printed word. Once distributed to a smaller population far less with the ability to read than is enjoyed today, sheets of parchment and later paper or whatever was available on which to write, tacked on trees, and pasted in windows, providing the latest news or warning or proclamation by reigning authorities. Then came the local town newspaper, often merely one sheet, then two and a new industry grew, including decimation of forests to feed the emerging appetite for greater and more comprehensive coverage of the latest happenings both locally and beyond and even across global borders. Larger urban areas, competing newspapers and broadsheets vied for subscribers. Today it is an amalgamation of disjointed voices, inscribed in print or emblazoned on televisions screens and bellowed from the incessant rant of radio emission and now form the commonly referred media.

Communication between individuals has been a critical connective link binding neighborhoods and increasingly populated areas. Certain experts claim that forms of what could be intelligible language may have been part of mankind's evolution over a quarter million years ago. Nonetheless, the distribution of words and viable distribution of information didn't truly become available until the printing press was invented as the words written before had been hidden away in archives. More often prepared by hand in monastery scriptoriums. It was then that learning to read was critical to any hope for advancement or understanding of what and when events affecting the populace could be revealed. In the era of pure speech transmission, it was a cacophony of rumors, half-truths, repeated myths, unknowing or overt lies and hearsay.

Within the the past several centuries , that panoply has become the lateral bread and butter of the journalist reporter and now the TV newscaster, the self-proclaimed pundit and regrettably too many members of local, state and national legislatures. Until methods of producing the verbal into the inscribed image became reasonably widespread, illiteracy was the norm for more than ninety-five percent of the world's population. Writing was the early centuries limited to scribes and trained priests serving the plethora of Gods in the empires of Egypt and the Middle East as well as the then primarily unknown and unexplored, exotic Orient. During the growth of the European continent, the ability to read was limited even among the nobility. In many parts of the world, learning to read became a danger to the existing government or monarchial power. To read gave the individual the opportunity to learn of other cultures – even more so – other philosophies and beliefs. Such personal power could lead to disagreement, then to dispute and eventually – revolution.

With the advent of the infant printing technology developed by Gutenberg and his colleagues during the medieval age, printing opened up a new and revelatory world to many more individuals. It led to the formation and distribution of information, ideas and in the minds of many, the seeds of dissent and eventual revolution. High-speed printing presses, photography and its use to add substance and greater receptivity for the words used, made the availability of news of the latest news dictated only by distance from the source and educational level. The written and later broadcasted word became both the substance of public knowledge and the basis for decision making. It was here the then print media and its later electronic colleagues, radio, television and now the Internet, became the heralds of old when messengers brought royal dictates to every town or hamlet and posted on the most familiar location.

Our founding Fathers were adamant in assuring that words would be the weapon of choice in maintaining the freedom of the people. Contrary to the literary and movie magnification of the role of the journalist, the heroic endeavors of the reporter and the absolute pledge of the media's primary duty to vouchsafe the flow of facts. That, disappointedly, has not been their history. From almost the inception of our government in 1790, the media in its early printed form has been allied to one political party or another, depending on the partisan or ideology of the particular publication's ownership. According to historians, that alignment was accepted as the norm and expected when viewing articles and editorial comments on the current party in power or its opposition. Although many reporters were in themselves dedicated to determining the truth and unappeasable desire to acquire the facts, they were often hobbled by the relationship between their employer and the political entity that often provide the needed income to continue the publication. This monetary connection may no longer exist, but the linkage remains in place.

Today the role of the media and its original purpose has become an entanglement of too many voices, all claiming to own the ensign of truth, the deliverer of fact and clarity. On the occasion of a major event, be it crime related or natural disasters and those caused by human error, social or political gathering of note or expected controversy, we will find the eyes and ears of the press and broadcast industry. TV cameras and the photographer's digital electronics. More recently, the now ever present video voyeur, the cell phone user. All are there to provide whatever form of fact they consider financially acceptable or ideologically conforming. When all is accessible to media outlets and the parasites of cell phone technology, what may be the actual facts and the truth will soon become a dissonant chorus of rumors and scuttlebutt.

A mélange of voices and visions that confuses, misleads and worse, provide the opportunity for those with a personal agenda to have the opportunity to create from the information provided, the truth as only they wish it to be presented. In essence, given the ability to lie or merely contribute distortion that either assuages their personal needs or serves the purpose of higher authorities. What causes the proclivity of some to conduct their professional role as specifically geared to their ambition or personal dislike or disagreement with the subject? Ego, desire to climb the ladder of professional acclaim and personal income. It can also be the nature of the individual being interviewed or the need to spend time on subjects considered lacking the revelatory impact of scandal or intrigue.

This is not meant to insult or deny the fine work many journalists and publishers have performed over the decades to embolden where the light of revelation was needed. They've provided at times the only channel of communication for the public to countenance with opinion and for the political, social and economic miscreants to be brought into view. Those members of the profession, however scattered throughout the globe and often working under very dangerous circumstances, they have been the guardians of free delivery of news and factual presentation. Disheartening as it is to we who understand and respect the ardor of the professional journalist in whatever facet of media they work, it has been revealed that certain ethical requirements of the function may have been curtailed in order to pursue advancement through public and political acclaim. It has been said that diplomats tell lies to journalists and then the speaker begins to believe what they read of their commentary. English author, Enoch Arnold Bennett wrote, "Journalists say things they know isn't true in the hope that if they keep saying it long enough it will be true." Ominously similar to a remark made by Adolph Hitler's propaganda chief, Josef Goebbels.

In the past fifteen plus years hundreds of dailies and numerous weekly newspapers have succumbed to both national economic vagaries and to possibly a greater degree the digital age. Many publications have found it difficult to create compelling content in their digital editions and competition from the myriad of Internet offerings on personal computers. `I pads' and the avalanche of cell phone opportunities has decimated a large part of the traditional reading public's interest in physical print. To the younger generation and their older compatriots, the speed and ease of merely viewing their handheld cell phones or iPads provides them an instant window to the world.

According to certain reports, only three major publications, the New York Times, the Wall Street Journal and the Washington Post are still outside the cusp of potential bankruptcy – at least according to their ownership. Other major urban area publications, Boston, Philadelphia, Las Vegas and Tampa, have drastically cut staff. Some have enveloped themselves in donation soliciting, tax exempt bosom of 501(c) (3) protection. Much as has had recently, the the Salt Lake City, UT Tribune, having materially trimmed staff and joining those seeking accessible tax deduction relief. The income flow besides subscriptions and advertising now includes donations by those acquiescing to the papers solicitation for help to survive. The Tribune's former advertising and printing relationship with the Church of Jesus Christ of Latter Day Saints publication of the Deseret News has been terminated. Referred to as the LDS or Mormon in brief form, and who also own the local NBC affiliate television station, KSL-5, formed an information conglomerate that had in the past caused inquiry about its claimed level of non-bias.

As a journalism major at a large Midwestern university, what seems like a century ago, I was not only taught but expressly counseled that if I were to pursue the profession, one rule was mandatory. Until someone or some group were to pay me expressly for my personal opinion or viewpoint on a subject I was to write about, I would be required to state only the facts, the substance of the subject itself and all relevant comments from pertinent observers or participants. Several times I'd submitted reports on local meetings I'd been assigned to cover as a classroom task. My use of the English language was marked as highly proficient, but my presentation as a reporter was flawed by insertions, either inadvertent or purposeful and minor, of my personal views. Several blistering comments by my professor and a reduced grade I did not quickly forget.

Today that professional ethic has been ridiculously abused and now readers must scan every article, every news alert with a degree of skepticism. The line between stated fact and possible commentary or opinion has blurred beyond reasonable acceptance, later suspect as having been prepared under a false premise. Many in the industry have become propagandists for particular political, economic or social activist influences. The have sold what may have been the initial visage of fairness for bot monetary and desired acclimation.

Still, in fairness to journalistic and associated reportorial disciplines, I herein state what I've always believed must be the hallmark of our right to know. *That if government is not subjected to constant inquiry, subjection of the governed is inevitable.* The loss and/or diminishment of so many newspaper legends is a sad reflection on the effects of a constantly changing technology. It is a situation that saddens many and marks a profound distancing from what was a heralded and much revered part of our emerging position on the global scene.

Yet, there do exist specific guidelines in absorbing news presentations or informative offerings, reading from one's Internet screen or perusing the many, and now even decreasing periodicals in print. In the newspaper industry, as with many magazines and tabloids, the headline is often the first and most lasting impression gained from only later cursory or momentary perusal of an article. It is a tool of the editorial desk to gain immediate attention, to assure the reader may linger a bit longer. Used just to strengthen the validity of of an article that lacks reasonable verification is not justifiable. It is to mislead, to prostitute the claimed unbiased intent of the article.

One of the most flagrant devices to hide the indistinct nature of truth or facts in any article is the constant use of the phrase "anonymous source" or "unidentified authority". This can often be the ideological signpost to indicate the desired opinions have been surreptitiously inserted within the article or broadcast presentation itself. This use of shadowy informants to which the reader or viewer is supposed to adhere to as fact are actually masks, hiding fact by inserting fiction. A modern day journalistic disclaimer, a curtain of potential secrecy to hide the actual truth while exciting interest and acceptance by all.

We are hopefully familiar with the concept of freedom of speech and its accompanying freedom of the press as a vital part of our constitutional rights. However, Thomas Jefferson had a somewhat limiting view of how that part should be phrased. In 1789, the Congressman James Madison has sent Jefferson an early draft of what would later become the Bill of Rights. Allow me a moment to quote Madison's initial draft; "The people shall not be deprived or abridged of their right to speak, to write or to publish their sentiments; and the freedom of the press is one of the great bulwarks of liberty, shall be inviolable." Jefferson approved of the "the declaration of rights" in general but added a caution to Madison. He suggested certain limitations as expressed in his recommended text; "The people shall not be deprived or abridged of their right to speak, to write or *otherwise* to publish anything *but false facts affecting injuriously the life, liberty, property or reputation of others or affecting the peace of the confederacy with other nations.*"

The question has often been asked since that time, "Freedom of speech for whom?" To bridge that gulf between the protection of the broadcaster's rights under the First Amendment and the public's right to access to controversial issues has been of great sufferance to the electronic media. Yet, it fails to approach to the continual complaint of defamation and near scurrilous commentary charged against the print media. Although an element of this article's approach to the subject of the abuse of facts, let us first discuss the electronic media's entry into the world of the printed word. The drastic decline in print news subscriber support fearfully presages a possible end of the vaunted and traditional newspaper in the coming years.

However, before we enter the technological maze of misstatement and misalliance that encompasses the entire broadcast industry, let us first discuss a subject often on the lips of those who have felt the barb and offensive spearhead of the media in general and print and electronic in particular. Two expressions that for many symbolize the right of the offended target; libel and slander. Without a possibly boring treatises on those two words, we should first determine what is meant by both. Regrettably, aside from the few newspaper columnists or cartoonist whose twisted version of facts has led he or she into the abyss of self-recrimination, the most prolific abusers of the freedom of speech in the area of slander or libel are the august members of the United States House of Representatives and Senate as they take place at the microphone on either floor. They seem to rival the members of the journalistic profession in exercising an intemperate use of language that so often borders if not unmistakably crosses over the lines of libel or slander. Although near that line, it is the rare journalist who will risk the inevitable legal actions were they to perpetrate such calumny.

Even more lamentable, the proclivity of legislators to carry such inane and juvenile behavior out to wherever a microphone, a television camera or cadre of contended journalist are gathered. The nature of their verbal insults insults, innuendos and blatant falsehoods would have in the 18th Century caused more sword or pistols duels than there would be sufficient open ground on which to carry out such responses to any claimed or inferred affront or slur. In a way, that early form of response to insult did seem to achieve lesser verbose or ill thought utterances and speech, people in those times may have been far more subdued when containing criticism of caustic riposte. This constitutional ability to openly defame or castigate through the archaic rules allowing such behavior is a shame the Congress has long supported and refused to cease either personally or by legislative adjudication.

In my latest book, "The Faultless Imperfection, A citizen's review of the US Constitution," I refer to this uninhibited speech privilege to some extent. For those subject to the ridicule or accusation of misdeed from the floor of Congress, it must further be noted that regardless of the veritably empty House or Senate chamber at the time of the comments, all said is being recorded in the Congressional Record. A massive compendium of legislative comment, discussion, legislative detail and more often than not, laudatory heaped on selected recipients or personalized condemnation of individuals, groups or actions found distasteful or inappropriate by the speaker. Simply stated, "Slander is defamation, utterances, spoken words that tend to damage the reputation or standing of another. Libel is ostensibly "false and malicious publication printed for the purpose of defaming another." There are numerous legal interpretations of certain acts that generally might fall within these two categories, but the case law and legal examples are far too voluminous to bore the reader at this time.

While the media will hover ever so rigidly at the protective wall of the First Amendment, the members of Congress are free to mock the possible legal ramifications of their speech directing attention to the constitution itself. A small part of Article I, Sect. 6, the first paragraph, states, referring to the legislators themselves, ". . . shall in all cases, except treason, felony and breach of peace, be privileged from arrest during their attendance at the session of their respective houses, and in going to and returning from the same; and for any speech or debate in either house during his continuance in office." Creating a 'get out of jail card' covering two violation of the laws that specifically refer to individual rights of those being denounced. History tells us that the intent in the early days of our nation's founding was to protect the then novice legislators from attack by mobs of disgruntled members of the opposing view of the speaker. Remembering there were still those opposed to the actual formation of this country in lieu of an altered relationship with the English king.

Inasmuch as the print industry and many of its corollary enterprises are literally submerging economically into one of the normal bathroom's salient features, we shall also wander over to the electronic side of the media. With the advent of photography and the immediacy of visual presentation via digital mechanisms and satellite assistance, what we see is purported to literally put the viewer at the scene, as he or she were there when it happened. Graphically illustrative of the actual event, but when manipulated as to positioning in an article, broadcast time, sequence of scenes and the inevitable editing room at all TV and radio stations, what is presented as real can actually be the progeny of electronic machination. The byline is the signature of the writer, a source for research as to who the individual is, who he or she are employed by, what group or organization or particular news reporting organization they represent.

It is the badge worn by the legitimate journalist. Regrettably, also the ill-deserved certification by those using assumed and often insufficient credentials to purvey themselves either as pundits or academic notables. There are many good members of the profession representing highly reputable news and information distribution. Sadly one aspect of this particular media does not enjoy that majority of superior talent. These mistakes in positioning by their employers at various media outlets and the editors assigned to direct their efforts are too often ill or poorly trained. In addition, they seek a prominence and attribution by the public as being superior in their professional acumen. The desire to succeed can too often edge the individual reporter, broadcast notable or news gatherer across that very dim, almost invisible line between the truth as it exists and the facts as they will fit the effect desired.

One striking demand for impartiality in what was said over the then new institution known as radio was the insistence on what was to become the "Fairness Doctrine," initiated by the Federal Communications Commissions (FCC) originally formed as the FRC or Federal Radio Commission when the broader Communications Act of 1934 was passed. Noted broadcast producer, Fred Friendly, a colleague of the famed radio voice, Edward R. Murrow, had an interesting commentary in his 1957 book, "The Good Guys, the Bad Guys and the First Amendment." Friendly went on to become president of the highly touted "CBS Reports." In his book he provided a brief history of an early legal confrontation between several radio stations, each demanding their right to broadcast how and when they preferred.

This particular disagreement as to rights of one station to extend its transmission hours in violation of the claim of another larger outlet's supposed control during that same period eventually ended up in the United States Supreme Court. As a result it brought about the congressionally augmented attempt at providing equality in presentation of differing viewpoints. Disheartening to its supporters, such an emphasis on assuring balanced coverage no longer exists. As with so many noble concepts, it was soon relegated to the archives of forgotten and ill implemented regulations.

With the proliferation of multiple chains of radio and television outlets, and the ability to access or control other competing voices within the same hearing range of the general public, fairness became an archaic term. Competition in ratings is the lifeblood of advertising revenue potential and its paramount concern and led broadcasting to the altar of the advertising dollar, making fairness irrelevant with the broadcast which more lately even includes the tax payer subsidized public broadcasting outlets. A very relevant insert, please. In April of 2020, Lester Holt, noted host of the evening, NBC news broadcast commented the fairness was an overrated expression. Ostensibly that he said it is not policy within the newscaster's purview to spend the time to allow both sides of an argument or controversy to be aired. That it is the broadcast right to use the current report and let later revelations provide an alternate theory or opinion. The blatant admission that the media consider it their right to report, to relay, to broadcast whatever they feel is necessary to achieve the results desired by the reporter or his or her employer.

Today we are belabored by the face emitting the voice that carries the news of the day in to our homes either visually on the TV or Internet screen or via radio transmission. The popularity of a number of such broadcast hosts, dictated of course by ratings, tend to indicate the level of acceptance that we the viewer, assess to his or her words. Now let us correct any misapprehension that we are talking of all the on screen personalities in all such medium. That is not the case. The newscaster, other than the interim program scheduling we see often during a broadcast day are merely providing the updated copy of events either in action at that time or have recently occurred. The line between fact and personal fictionalization finally crossed the line with little or no attempt to bring the expression fairness back into the vernacular when cable programing became the primary news distributor. It has been shown, regardless the need to reinstitute some degree of impartiality in daily print and electronic media, would be a daunting task.

Briefly there are two types of news program hosts; the network originated and prime time channel news offerings and the "commentators." Those who use news items or current event accounts as platforms for their personal interpretations and doctrinal opinions. It is this over profusion of self-styled pundits and flaunters of falsehoods offered as erudite discussion that so distorts fact from fictionalizing. It is to the shame of both newsprint and broadcast media hierarchy that required immediately at the beginning of each of such presentations, simply state the comments and observation of the following individuals are their own or as directed by their employer. The common dialogue between channel news and commentary programs are laden with like opinions and agreements with the host's obvious bias toward one side of any controversial subject or situation. This then lends credence to and a subtle way of inserting the specific ideological thinking and intent of either the speakers themselves or whomever they answer to for their employment.

With the almost total exclusion of other national events or attention warranted incidents, only two primary situations have dominated the print and broadcast media during the year 2020. To the greatest measure, the pandemic has caused increasing areas of serious illness, its affected economic downturns, normal social interruption and tragically, so many deaths. It is viewed for what it is, a great misfortune and extremely trying time for the population and those heroic medical health workers and facilities who constantly battle the effects of this newly introduced virus. With the coupling of the violent protests resulting from the tragic and improper death of a black man at the hands of a police office in late March of 2020 as well as later instances involving law enforcement, for a time it was media's position to place an emphasis on what they referred to as probable law enforcement misfeasance.

Let us put that subject aside for the moment please, as it will unfortunately be incremental in our discussion of the frustration oriented folly during the ensuing rampant and destructive series of public protests. The printed word has become disingenuous at best and the current dissolution of so many newspapers and magazines, has for what was over two centuries, our window to the ever expanding nation and the equally emerging world. Too many media resources have become too often conveyers of near propaganda on behalf of the political bent of each paper's ownership and internal management.

For so many years, the New York Times, the famed "Gray Lady of journalism as that highly touted publication was well-known, has itself become subject to criticism and skepticism as to its verities'. In recent years it, along with its colleague Washington Post and its similar West Coast publishing giants have become producers of numerous articles bearing serious examination. Regrettably, a number of these columnists seem to form a mélange of individuals, oriented to a leftist bent, familiar to those who have studied Marx and other Communist spokespersons. Commentary by those with proven academic or professional acumen or well identified expertise in a subject remain the mainstay of radio and television talk programming and becoming in recent years strongly progressive and extremely leftist in viewpoint. The pertinent channel program hosts themselves seem to continually minimize or totally eliminate any disputing rebuttal.

These type of expanded on air dialogues were supposedly designed to bring new and expanded thought on many subjects to a public having less opportunity to pursue such topics themselves. It was a form of education to those desirous of expanding their own understanding of the new, the interesting and the valuable to one's personal well-being and health. However, when it became a litany of political and social diatribe, providing only one singular viewpoint and no opportunity at the same time to disagree or counteract comment given as fact, that indefinable line between factual and falsehood, informative and bias infested has been crossed.

Thus arises the counter voices, the separate radio outlets and television channels that offer opposing or disclaiming opinions. With the rising tendency of the three mainstream network groups, NBC, CBS and ABC to enter this miasma of directed and apparently biased presentation of certain news items and personalities, see a continuing violation of their declared professional oath of fairness in coverage and reporting. They were always thought to be the clearest voice of objective reporting clean of personal bias or suspect prejudice. But with the advent of increased competing news channels, it has become, and will continue to be, a war of words and biased approach to each news item. It forces the listener and viewer to determinate wherein lies the truth of any presentation. What is even more disturbing is an apparent intent to deny the truth and the obvious avoidance of presenting any material that the ownership finds in conflict with their personal and political interests. A sad commentary in itself as it diminishes the concept of fairness in providing the news and related information.

The most salient impression one garners from watching to any extent any of the three major network news programming, coupled with the mainstream channel TV news productions, could be of a scripted dialogue, perfected and manifested hate – a full blown exhibition of a total disregard for fairness in presentation. It seems to show in their facial grimaces as they announced the latest charge against the then incumbent resident of 1600 Pennsylvania Ave. during the 2016 campaign of tenure of 2017-2021. As to be fair, Trump's political opponent had also received a modest but often relatively benign share of verbal abuse from a small segment of the broadcast industry. It must be assumed that no fair minded individual wishes to see any measurable restrictions on the freedom of the press as guaranteed in the First Amendment. Yet, the fairness doctrine, as referred to earlier, still has cogent meaning. It should remain one of the pillars of strength supporting the rights of the journalist and broadcaster to pursue their craft, but with an adherence to the quality and equality of presentation. For all purposes however, this proposed standard of equality has been left in the rubble of political conflict.

Apparently in the journalistic profession, printed sarcasm, verbal vitriolic emanation is not the exclusive province of only one side of the political spectrum It is difficult to determine if this vilification actually demonstrates the speaker's personal opinion and feelings or is a directed imagery of inner rage and a public display of enmity by those who control the broadcast facilities from somewhere on high. When hate is the visible or subliminal emotion, truth becomes a secondary concern. If this expression of apparent loathing of any subject with which the reporter or columnist and the broadcast personality is in compliance with the dictates of the media's ownership, then our information source is being controlled. And when controlled, the First Amendment freedom of speech becomes what those unknown financial influences say it is. Freedom – at the listener's personal loss and cost.

As an aside, this writer was fascinated with what could be one of the more telling anecdotes related to the function of the journalist. As the Nazis were assaulting the beleaguered London populace by air in 1940, the BBC, the British Broadcasting Corporation, previously considered the staid producer of somewhat aesthetic and boring arts, literature and other cultural pursuits, was enlisted to become the voice of a resisting England. One of the well-known Manchester Guardian's writers, R.T. Clark had joined the newly formed group of reporters and broadcast personnel. He is reported to have announced to the assemblage about their function, "Well brothers, now that war has come to us, your job is to tell the truth, and if you aren't sure it is, don't use it." A maxim that should be emblazoned over ever press room door, every broadcast booth and on the front of every television camera while in operation. The current mélange of contended media voices must understand, their bias, lies, subterfuge of valid and required information has almost destroyed the past credibility they once enjoyed. Simple stated, get your act in order. Remember, when there is no light of fact, all men are blind. But to deliver the light is to provide truth to some and reality to others.

Chapter 9

What of Tomorrow?

The next observation may well excite some interest in those who enjoy a reintroduction of more recent history. It involves the ongoing introduction of a racial element in public conversations, medical offerings and all social, economic or physical confrontations now occurring. Race as a word has been taken hostage by numerous special interest groups and politically obsessed activists. The actual word `race' can refer to a tribe, a clan, a bloodline, descent, strain, breed, ancestry, parentage, ad infinitum. In general terms, can also refer to nations, people or folks. The increasing number of incidents involving law enforcement officers and black or African-American individuals resulting in injury and too often death to the person accosted or being pursued has engendered a massive outrage in both black and more liberally minded communities. Time to review.

Race has been the natural decision utilized by mankind since the Cro-Magnon may have viewed the emerging Neanderthal, wondering what this new introduction into its world could be or could affect the viewers own personal existence. The meeting of different human figures, possibly of a different skin hue, size, facial construction. And most importantly, speaking in a fashion not understandable by the viewer. Again, a personal decision will be made. To accept this newcomer, to allow the entrance of the stranger into one's own environment. When mankind had become more acclimated to movement beyond his own domain, to know there may be others, unlike those of his or her familiar setting, such chance encounters become the normal aspect of travel.

In the minds of the unaware arose the specter of slavery, an unexpected occurrence that needed titling. To the modern, supposed savant, slavery was the result of racial disparity and bias. In the field of academic immaturity, this immediate conclusion was at least reaching beyond sustainable boundaries of then known facts. The slave, whether as hostages resulting from conflict, indentured servants, based on indebtedness, the use of conquered tribes and at times, whole nations of people, was part of the trade, commerce and inevitable residue of war and conquest. The Hebrew was not enslaved from a racial consideration. They were available from earlier conquests, or had become part of the normal population increase until their services under restraint became more economically feasible.

The Mongols under the Genghis Khan, Attila the Hun, Alexander and more modern history, the militaristic nature of Roman rule, collected humans as the spoils of success in warfare. In many instances, what to do with this added population? To feed them, give them housing, provide the very basis needs would become incomprehensible. Thus, they would become the unpaid, minimally supported workers to effect improvement in the structural and social life of the victor. In the Mideast, people of the same ethnic background, by others when overridden by stronger, more aggressive tribes or neighboring nations, became slaves. At times, these hostilities were waged with the desire, and at times the need to acquire riches and property. During those eras, definition of property included humans.

As travelers and explorers moved from continent to continent, slavery was an accepted part of many of the cultures visited. In Africa, tribal wars and conflicts resulted in the capture and enslavement of other who, in the main were of similar ethnicity and color and often of similar cultures. It was the Introduction of the non-African trader, the merchant found a situation from which they could profit. Dominant tribal chiefs in the areas were more than eager, for personal gain, to assist in acquiring additional individuals through surprise and violent means to fulfill the new slave trader's needs. Indentured servants were common in the growing colonial America. Many brought in from Ireland, England, Scotland and parts of Europe to satisfy past debts or as penalty for minor crimes. Thus, importation of slaves, in the minds of many agricultural interests, was not that far afield from current uses for bonded individuals. The slave trade prospered in the prerevolutionary War period. Only to become a major political and social awareness with the installation of the new constitution and disagreement with the practice in more industrial northern colonies.

Regardless of its basic etymology the word race has been bandied about irresponsibly and has become the semantic crutch for the rationally infirmed. Unfortunately, the singular interpretation of the word race by the social and political activist, refers only to the Negro, the black man, the African American. The existence of said racial disparity and assault is rarely mention when referring to other minorities – "those other people" in the minds of the uninformed and ideologically twisted. Of course racism exists, it has for centuries and regrettably may for still a time off. It requires individual, social and institutional removal which can only come from a unified approach. One that the vagaries of activist comment and the lethargy of local, state and national legislature refuses to accomplish.

Notwithstanding, the ostensible leadership in the black community seems to immediately take a fallback position from rational consideration concerning any incident, any contestation, verbal or physical and any subjective decision relating to the care, administration or recourse involving any minority. No time is spent attempting to resolve any such occurrence or to seek consideration of various aspects of what has happened or becomes contentious. It is that initial striking of the polemical match and the fire of dispute suddenly emerges.

As a result we have the "Black Lives Matters" movement, along with its less obvious colleague, "Antifa" or the mixed collage of malcontents. The plethora of protests has afflicted the national consciousness with violence, damage to property, injury and deaths of several innocent bystanders. Regardless of whether the accused are found guilty of improper assault or even murder in varying degrees, when and if the matter is resolved and the accused offenders found not culpable one salient factor always remains, have those in the body of such protests or the leadership ever apologized. Ever signaled remorse for the tragedy of innocent civilians being injured or killed for no creditable reason? Simply, no.

Still remembered by many, the infamous Tawana Brawley fiasco of 1987 in New York City when she was found with racial epithets painted on her body, and she claimed police officers had committed the gruesome offense. Immediately the shrimp figured black activist, the Rev. Al Sharpton, known for exacerbating any situation n involving blacks and whites, became the loudest author of a continuous supposed litany of white oppression when he jumped into the fray. Then it was discovered she had been out with a boyfriend, far beyond her parents imposed time limits. Did Sharpton or any of the other black activists apologize or the media make a pronounced revelation of the actual facts? They did as has happened too often in such instances, immediately waged a war of words, condemnation of supposed perpetrators or targets of blame with little or no substance. Or in fact, did the young woman herself ever admit remorse for having created this blatant fraud? Never! Yet it did provide a misdirected media an excuse for immediate decrying of racial inequality and the need to place the blame on someone or some unknown organization, regardless the paucity of facts at the time.

True, the past history of assaults on member of the black community and too frequently the lack of immediate and thorough investigation and pursuit of those possibly responsible has become synonymous with the ever increasing present racial divide. When the Duke University Lacrosse team members were falsely charged with sexual misbehavior by a paid, stripper, prostitute, another activist without portfolio, Jesse Jackson rode into town decrying the racism that was present. After a trial that exonerated the young men, evidence that the woman lied and misfeasance charges against the local prosecuting attorney forced that individual to resign, was there any apology? Never!

When the Rev. Wright, noted as pastor to a former president, spewed his hate and "*G..Damn* America" vituperation constantly, even selling CDs of his bile filled anti-white sermons. Was there ever any apology by any black leadership? No, or that his bigoted ideology was not the basic feelings of other like members of the cloth and the many principally black congregations throughout the United States.? Never? When a histrionic African American Harvard professor raged and ranted after reports to police mistakenly indicated someone was attempting to break into the man's house. Again it was racial profiling. It was the "honky white" doing harm to the poor black man. When facts revealed the officer was merely responding to a call by the man's neighbor, and the supposed Ivy League College intellectual had actually lost his house keys while traveling, what was the result? Intercession? Or just another political `photo op' when the then first

African American president hosted a gathering with the "racially offended" professor and the police officer, making for a well utilized propaganda opportunity and nothing more. But those are incidents of the past, excessively covered with the tainted nature of biased observers adding fictional interpretation to fact.

As another marked example for certain ethnic sources to refuse criticism even when well-deserved, would be the numerous NFL and NBA professional athletes too often found guilty of repeated drug offenses, domestic abuses and in a number of instances, even serious criminal acts. So where is the moral basis, the so-called required equality that blacks demand when their actions and misdeeds warranted those brief suspensions, almost meaningless at times with minimal deductions from their exaggerated salaries and then back into the fold of their fellow athletes? With the predominance of the black athlete in professional basketball and football and increasing minority composition of Major League Baseball, we must also face the impressionable impact of that demographics on our youth.

It has been broadly accepted that our youth tend to model their efforts and personal behavior on the images of high-profile and successful athletes. They, along with various celebrities', form the role model concept afforded them through their media promoted elevation as the desired symbol of accomplishment. Examples of success over early difficulties, a supposed valuable lesson for young people still attempting to move from childhood into the demanding world of the adult. The well-publicized statements of support by many of the professional teams, including using their public imagery both individually and when on the court or the field, emboldens the Black Lives Matter movement, regardless of the recurring violence and destruction that has marked that entities rise as a major activist organization.

The question is posed, what is the appropriate posture to be taken by these young athletes, male and female? To be in concert with the need for all to recognize and deal with our failure to properly integrate the minority population into the full benefits and participation in our nation is laudable. It seems however, that the displays of kneeling while the national anthem is played or when TV cameras are focused on them is not just a show of any honest belief but perhaps merely a show of their vaunted position in society and elevated stature. Is not the behavioral development of the child the express responsibility of the parent, or in absence of same, the most available counselor, teacher, coach or religious leader? It is a quandary that only time and the efforts of those closest to the younger generation can solve. What then should be the response to the arrogance of posture and demand to purvey their personal position by these professional athletes be from parents who are the primary dictators and managers of the children's upbringing and training?

When Barack Hussein Obama was elected president, the first black person to gain that vaunted position, it was conjectured this heralded the rising of the minorities on the national scene. Expectations were rampant, the black segment of the population as well as a number of other minority leadership, may have felt their time had come. They ability to take a rightful place in both the social realm but importantly, among local and national leadership roles. I feel these anticipations may have fallen far short of their desires and needs. Race was a dominant theme in the 2008 election. It marked a salient point in promoting the young, charismatic, well-educated and effective speaker whose father himself had been a governmental activist in his native Kenya.

Little mention seemed to be made of Obama's Midwestern raised, collegiate educated mother, Stanley Ann Dunham. A specialist in anthropology, holder of a Masters and PhD degrees, who married a fellow student from Kenya, later divorcing him and marrying an individual from Indonesia. All such details are available on the various Internet sites. However, the factor apparently of little interest was, his mother was white. Thus, did this ethnic and genetic mixture diminish or magnify the former president's allure or abilities. Evidently of little consequence according to the many writings, biographies, and laudatory explanations of his rise to power. The emphasis was, at times, solely, he's the first black to achieve this height. He is a symbol of the black experience.

This is not to criticize him, other than disagreement with certain of his policies and his apparent disregard of the then apparent needs of the black community. The purpose of this brief aside is to further dampen the ardor of those who may feel that being black is the only consideration when equating achievement as against probable racial bias. Such exclusive reasoning overtly or inadvertently disregards the many mixed racial formats including Hispanic, Middle Eastern and the entirety of the Pacific and Caribbean population, many of whom share a heritage with the principal black racial origin.

No to the serious needs for support elements to law enforcement and security, there are public services whose membership need their levels of training, equipment and pay elevated to a degree that it attracts and maintains the best. We require a designated course and time of study for the profession of medicine and similar demands on time and effort for those desiring to enter the legal profession. Each of them are subject to ongoing review by their peers and when errors, whether accidental or inadvertent or proven a direct fault, there is penalty. Perhaps censure, suspension of practicing licenses. Even more stringent, those penalties can result in criminal prosecution. Both professions hopefully preserve life as in the case of medicine and for attorneys, possibly holding the fate of clients facing judicial process.

The police, fire and social service professionals are assigned the protection and care of the public and in the instance of the social worker the specific safeguarding of our children and their families and alertness and watchfulness for their needs and safety. For the police officer candidate, the first step is the application to and vetting for employment. It is the method of selecting candidates from a pool of applicants desiring a worthwhile and respected occupation or to the opposite, identifying someone possibly seeking a position that could allow them a status of authority and public awareness never before attained. This particular desire to achieve an undeserved stature is often the beginning of the overly reactive individual, someone whose inner emotional and social frustrations are manifested in violent reaction when pressured. For the fire service applicant, the eventual pressure and trauma when facing the devastating and often deadly consequences of blaze after blaze, can also create emotional and emotional turmoil on and off duty. They too, need ongoing care and attention to the rigors of their functions and the effect on their personal psyches.

Beginning salaries that are at best commonly low, unnecessarily forcing the new employee into potential financial distress. An added stress that can seriously affect his or her performance when faced with the unexpected in dealing with an unsuspected or problem situation. Too often abbreviated training because of costs, requires review and better yet, expansion into additional topics; identifying possible mental health conditions when observing erratic or disturbing reactions when accosted. How social norms have changed, the particular cultural variances in areas where assigned, the list of critical considerations is endless when training to deal with other humans.

Voiced by many experts is the critical need for continuous and thorough psychological review of police, fire safety and first responders to assure both the ability to control potential emotional conflict and the burdens of their functions. Staff psychologists at all home bases for such personnel should be mandatory. Review of past and reoccurring incidents involving personnel conflicts, unacceptable behavior or noncompliance with agreed procedures and training. True, such assistance can be expensive, but pre judgement of situations and occurrences can save lives or injuries, both to personnel and the public. More so, the lessening of public condemnation of actions of individual employees that could have been avoided or recognized earlier.

Yet, the absence of such professionals at every stage of application, skills determination, training and the crucial early years on the street creates a major flaw in the required ongoing review of any first responder during the of the recruitment, evaluation, training and duty assignments. As they are human, it is the responsibility of their supervisors to assure each and every one enduring the pressure felt on the street must be part of every departmental staff. As important, the same rigid standards required of all members of the command chain in any department. Individuals equally trained and observed, dedicated to being fair in their review of incident reports, actionable events and the need to be thorough and speedy in all such inquiries.

When question arises as to if that professional line has been crossed, immediate action to assure the victims, if any, and the public that the matter has gained full attention by those in authority. Here is where a share of the endemic fault lies. It must also be put directly on the shoulders of the police departmental hierarchy from the training officers to the unit commanders and upward through the highest administrative and operational ranks. Still, even before the challenging o designated responsibility, it is local municipal authorities who also must be accountable – the Mayors, City Manager and whatever elected council conducts the people's business.

When these elected legislators and city or town management fail to be alert and actively deal with potential and occurring problems concerning the relationship between first responders and the public, they violate their oaths as `servants' of the people who selected and placed them in their positions. Political necessity invariably overcomes a more reasoned and measured approach as to their next response or needed action. However, in too many cases it is the media who begins the vocalization of public outrage and in concert with the broadcast segments, become the the heralds of demanded action without any pause to investigate and determine what has happened and where the fault may lie. And in turn it is the local political figures who will instantly either hide behind self-serving rhetoric to defend themselves from criticism or leap into the media constructed fray, blaming the nearest potential target just to gain greater voter approval.

Professions dealing directly with people of all economic, ethnic and cultural backgrounds must continually be updated on changes in community temperatures, social pressures or whatever has been noted as bringing unrest to the residents therein. The need to provide such cultural and community relations desired competency throughout the officer's employment tenure by defined and rigorously maintained schedules of procedural and legal updates as well as changing situations in any community or assigned duties. Want to place blame?

Merely look to local, state and national legislators who have consistently failed to recognize where much of this problem lies and have placed a dollar value on the votes they can garner from those to whom any tax increase is an assault on their support of the incumbents.

For the social worker and those dealing on a daily basis with the public government offices where the stress of acquiring motor vehicle licenses, local tax questions or any other provided services, requires courteous and concerned employee interaction with inquirers. Inquirers who may already be facing their own personal or professional tensions. Unless well trained, decently paid and exhibiting a continued recognition of the sensitive nature of their relationship with the public there will be a constant belief that the government, local, state or federal officials hold their constituent public in disdain.

The cost budgeting insistence by authorities of overloading child welfare and general public social care representatives with excessive caseloads portends missed opportunities to correct various domestic and child care problems. Forcing such a situation denies those in need the professional care and attention and thus becomes an act of misfeasance on the part of the local and state agencies assigned operational control. Too often it is the local and state legislators who fail the very public to whom they look for tax income and greater political acceptance. To many of them, the totals spaces at the bottom of columns on the legislative ledger sheet reflects votes, not dollars and cents.

This essay is not intended to defend without reservation the past history of law enforcement in its many forms and specific responsibilities. We owe a continuing support of the police personnel whose daily efforts provide us a degree of safety and assurance of assistance that would not be available otherwise. However, the shame of past and current misdeeds, improper and deadly misapplication of their skills cannot forgive those who have been and are seemingly still potentially guilty of such horrendous acts resulting in the injury or death of individuals. Many who were not guilty of any offense and others to which the excessive reaction of the arresting or pursuing officer was totally uncalled for and procedurally insupportable. These, hopefully fewer than the critics would contend, are those who must be removed from the departments and preferably never allowed original admission based on noted situations evolving from effective psychological workups. A recommendation that will cost more tax funds and bring howls of displeasure from both economically stressed tax payers and vote soliciting politicians.

We must understand that fear kills imagination and frustration stifles desire to attempt the formerly unattainable. Our current national administration's inadequate policies regarding the recommendations contained in this work seem to have become the standard in many local jurisdictions. I am from an age now treated with disregard and at times, disdain. Sadly I've come to realize that despair dwells in the wilderness of man's mind when he or she have been discarded by a younger and more unforgiving generation. Thomas Jefferson said it best regarding those who seek the votes of their fellow citizens: "When man first considers elective office, the rottenness begins." In the mid-1800s, government was fully contended to be, by consent of the people. Today, we are required to seek consent of the government to exercise our constitutional rights. Our current congressional morass and presidential insufficiency, has proven that politics is the gangrene that saps the moral fiber of our nation.

The social and ethical dilemma of the African American in today's society is most evident in any review of the ranks of professional football, basketball and to a degree in major league baseball. The number of black athletes, wined and dined, courted as early as their prior high school years, has increased to a level that in many instances, some critics will contend almost eliminates a fair qualification of talent and opportunity for many Caucasian youths or other minorities. The expense of matriculating, maintaining and fielding this growing number of minority athletes, can beggar the imagination. Yet, one to three years and the black athlete and a few of his fellow teammates, immediately jump into the professional selection pool, usually declaring the just wants to earn the big money to "buy their momma a new house and make her life easier."

Noble as that sounds, many collegiate football and basketball teams have seen their athletic program in those sports, decimated by the early withdrawal of their prized athletes, many black, for the rich professional pastures. One does not want to demean these young people merely seeking the better life for themselves and often for family who supported them so strongly during their youth. But why cannot the team spirit, the locker room comradery that melds such athletic teams into true families away from the individual homes. A unique ethical and moral covenant demanded of all fellow team members to respect one another and particularly all those people who are part of the fan base and most importantly their closest personal relationships – family, wives or other associates.

When a member of a collegiate or professional the team moves astray and creates undesirable imagery for the very profession that has garnered them economic fortune and fame, it is an insult to the team, his family and his ethnic background if he or she are of minority extraction. It allows those with innate racial bias to use such actions or misdeeds to support their already prejudiced nature, It extends hate into fertile areas where individuals, until such misdeeds, now had not given such thoughts any clear interest into the nature of the offense. They and their particular club affiliation from management to ownership, become targets for the inveterate bigot to pursue.

In the decades of abuse by law enforcement of every level, too often in the execution of their duties, an environment of fear and distrust of both the law officers themselves but also the local governmental authorities who have protected and at times countenances such behavior. Out of this era of purposeful bias, the minority individual, his or her associates and friends, family members, all were infected with the innate belief that those wearing the badge and carrying the weapon are the enemy. It is a near impossible image to erase from the minds of those who have been abused, mischaracterized as a criminal element and forced to suffer injustice at the hands of local law enforcement, the prosecutorial process and even at the bar of justice. It will take time, perhaps an inordinately large amount of time. More so a coordinated effort by all the related entities. Most importantly both national and local legislatures of both parties and those clarion cries for equality and justice above all which have more lately become just vituperative carrion dialogue.

Unfortunately, we are now faced with a new abundance of pseudo news outlets; that growing plethora of cell phone reporters who never fail to electronically record any occurrence, however benign when submitted to the local television outlets or headline obsessed print media. As a result, no action, no circumstance, however needing assistance, rather than bystander filming, is safe from what has become the bane of objective reporting of any situation. A major concern with all these cell phone videos, how and when they were recorded. From what angle, at what distance and was the recording altered in any manner, either by the phone user or eventually when finding its way to the television production room?

The fomenters of these crowd eruptions are either trained or paid employees of the particular group wanting such turmoil or that small cadre of younger disenchanted individuals who too often consider their own inability to be an effective part of society or any acceptable or traditional cause. Now what of the majority of the crowd, those who honestly believe their efforts are part of the noble heritage gained from rights granted in the First Amendment; "or the right of the people peaceably to assemble, and to petition the Government for redress of grievances." And this is the basic premise of such protests by the sincere, violence rejecting believer. It has not value to the assigned protest agitator or his or her control and fun ding source.

Unfortunately, the possibility that many of the younger members of such crowds may not have rationally reviewed the particular event or cause or desired change never occurred. They either accept the media's pronouncement and that of synthetic experts without they, themselves, taking the time to look closely into the details of what they are emotionally urged to protest. Or could be their need to conduct their own review of the situation is overtaken by the influence of fellow advocates, many times within the collegiate student body atmosphere. Worse yet, instigation and preplanned arguments by paid or activist agitators to develop groups of similarly thinking individuals to present a greater crowd synergy.

We hear the constant and justifiable cries for equality and diversity and justice. No one appears to have the resolution of each of those critical points in satisfying the greatest number of complaints. Diversity is necessary so long as it does not create division the assessment of rights. Equality in any undertaking means a level playing field but not the sole choice of referees and game rules by just a single group. For justice to be provided it must first be administered with the full consideration of its effect on all who are involved. The challenge of dealing with racism in its many overt, assumed or supposed forms is possibly the most daunting and troubling predicament this nation faces now and for the foreseeable future. Defining what is a racist term or inference, designating clearly racially influenced actions is a confusing riddle. It requires consideration and patient review, all in the face of a most emotionally intense situation when questioned as to being fact or personal opinion.

Even the physical individualization of what is politically correct demanded African American is usually a black man, or black female or black child. Not dark brown or brownish or darker than most normally swarthy physiques. Thus the definition is the code word for either someone who is different, a person not part of traditional social structure or a fully identifiable member of the human species. In his book, "The Story of My Life," by famed attorney and human rights activist, Clarence Darrow, there appears a fascinating comment that might best be described as a far more acceptable of identifying anyone as he wrote; "I was in New York, and a committee of Negroes came to see me regarding an upcoming case involving one of their organization's members. I knew they were Negroes because they told me so. In color and intelligences they were like many of the white men I know."

It was a simple statement of attitude. They'd introduced themselves as they accepted they were, ethnically and he accepted their personal identification as they stated. He expressed no predisposed decision as to their positions life or their color or any prior determination as to their worth and standing within the society of mankind. If we could assume this type of constant nonjudgmental evaluation, could not the traditionally expected tension between two parties of different ethnic origin could be greatly diminished and eventually eliminated. As my time on this beleaguered planet is far shorter than most, I leave the resolution of this cancer of conscious or unrecognized prejudice to those younger and hopefully more erudite and perceptive than I have been.

Chapter 10

Rule of Law, Abused in Court

We are taught the law should not be controlled by emotion nor is compassion written within the lettering of those laws. As cold and seemingly cruel to observers as this might be the law is designed and must function as an equalizing format for all who appear before the courts. Without this equality for the accused, whether innocent or guilty, or having become enmeshed in situations they should have avoided, the law is direct. The structure by which actions are governed by the prosecutorial, defense and judicial process is further delineated, if not at times either misconstrued or misapplied. The defense may utilize emotion and compassion. The background and specific conditions of prior life can be part of the argument against any guilty verdict. However, it is the role of the prosecutor to present the bare facts as have been gathered, the pertinent factors – the motive – that may have generated the act. Anything less on either side is to deny justice.

After having moved through the bramble of legal prohibitions and its inevitable process, the final episodes usually involve entering the domain, or to some critics, the lair of the judicial system in our country. Of the three divisions of our governmental system, the third as referred to in *Article III* of the constitution is the judiciary. Provided initially at the founding of our country was the Supreme Court with seven members, later expanded to nine as it sits today. The court's responsibilities and functions are enumerated in *Sects. 1 & 3* of that article. Directly the constitution positions the Supreme Court as the highest legal authority in the nation, providing final legal decisions on all matters presented.

The fledgling congress then allowed formation of lower courts titled appeals or circuit and district courts.

Just below the Supreme Court are the 12 Appeals, or referred to as Circuit Courts. Political activists contend the 9th District Court which includes California and the other two West Coast, states reflect a dominant Democratic number of appointees. As does the 10th District, encompassing Utah and Wyoming and what is often called the intermountain west; as does the 1st. 4th and the District of Columbus, serving strictly the nation's capital city. Yet, the 2nd district with New York as its hub, and the 4th containing Pennsylvania and New Jersey, have a majority of Republican appointed justices as well as the remaining districts. So regardless of critics on both side of the aisle, the Appeals Court districts dominated by Democrat leaning justices can be substantiated by the mathematics. Just below those figures are district courts and then the various state and Federal District courts each having their specific jurisdiction and normally dealing with particular cases assigned them.

Beyond the stature and position of the High Court are those numerous individual Supreme Court judicial assignments covering smaller communities or less populated rural confines. Too often the judicial bench in certain smaller areas is held by an individual with limited judicial and even legal expertise. The insufficient compensation, lack of appropriate staff and the wherewithal to conduct any degree of research restricts these jurists ability to more broadly scope the range of those particularly complex cases that may be presented. Television and novelists will use these economic and resource impediments to cast unfavorable light on the more provincial authorities and their somewhat local tradition governing manner of handling a variety of cases. Although there are instances of impropriety and outright misfeasance in dealing with accused individuals, they are hopefully rare and become more the additional fodder in originally weak scripts and impoverished drama foisted on the viewing public by the programmers.

If any discussion of the Rule of Law can encompass volumes of often indecipherable verbiage and totally obtuse jargon, invariably the final decision in any matter lies with the courts however locally oriented. The most voiced concern of late asks, does political association or partisan ideology affect the opinion and decision process in any part of the judiciary at whatever level? Yes, it can and possibly does, if only inadvertently inserting its limiting perspective into some judgements which this writer sincerely hopes is infrequent. Yet the rising claims of political influence in court decisions, especially at the Supreme Court level is most reflected in role of interpretation of a claim and raises doubt as to the constitutionally expected separation between the legislative and judicial process.

In recent years, decisions from the court at numerous levels have seemed to wander into actual rewording of the original law or statute being contested. Within these court judgements have appeared an apparent reconstituting of the intent of the original petition or directive being litigated. If such diversion from its constitutionally mandated function and responsibility does occur, such actions violates the very basis of our governmental structure. It interjects bias and preference into a process that must be kept inherently free of such interference and separate from inclusion with any other body or agency.

The law is the adhesive that binds our sometimes fragile democracy together, allowing its basic premise, equality under that same law to assure personal freedom for all. When a piece of legislation, a dissent issued against a standing law or statute comes before the any court, it is not the position or right of that body or individual justice to consider a rewording or variant to what is presented as the actual verbiage. Passionate pursuit of those legal factors that fail to fulfill the petitioner's request or need stems from the laws initially created upon and upon which any prosecution or defense or judicial petition and effort to resolve must be based. Without the primary statement of law in place, the petitioner, the defendant or prosecutor can seek a realistic. However, this often requires the issue to be remitted back to the pertinent legislature whose mandate is the preparation, discussion and decision on specific law making. In total, it is a process that holds together the frailty of man's actions and their results.

So many feel in today's world that we are in the midst of major epics in human history. A thinking that mankind is experiencing a social and moral revolution unparalleled in scope and intensity. That unrest and turmoil throughout the globe affects all people and their institutions wherever located. In this country it is particularly freedom of speech, religion and political ideologies. To some it is possible man is entangled in a vast and complex web he himself, unknowingly and possibly cleverly designed and boldly spun. The loyal church attendee feels religion is the foundation of the needed and required moral and ethical basis for any civil society. Elsewhere, others declare an equal right to be as free a spirit as emotion and the situation will allow. The practice of any theological belief and the freedom to both participate and proselyte to others their strict adherence is one of the more emotion enflaming convictions. If restrained by law or social disregard, where then are the more religiously oriented to go to find the desired truth of their personal existence? How can the political advocate speak their cause or the free spirit revel in being heard? Where does this thin line between freedom to decide and the required obedience to any particular ideology or theological doctrine lie in the face of opposing viewpoints? Specifically when does the common man find the definition of what is real and what is religious myth or recited dogma? We will enter that hornets' nest of potential emotional unrest and confrontation, next.

Chapter 11

When Words Become Human Law

Before the wrath of every individual with the slightest belief in some religious doctrine or feel they are advocate of whatever theology I may discuss herein, allow me to preface the following.

It is not the purpose of this part of my essay to debate or dispute whether the numerous revisions of the Holy Bible are true recitations of the history and development of the basic precepts of Christianity or solely a work of fiction. The various legends or fables provided by writers of an age almost all never dwelled in during the time of the principal figures, Jesus Christ, later Mohammed and even more recent, the LDS founder, Joseph Smith. I have no deep academic knowledge of the ancient Torah, nor can I articulate to any degree as to the verity of the Book of Mormon or the Islamic Koran. My familiarity such subjects is far too limited to proffer any definitive judgement on what is holy writ in any religious doctrine or could just be the figment of an ardent follower's devotion or a misled belief by its adherents.

This chapter targets the religious leadership, the priests, bishops, pastors, ministers, congregant proclaimed or self-endowed prophets. The many who follow a particular doctrine or have a firm conviction of a particular faith or denominational teaching, I wish every constitutional and legal ability to continue their personal reliance on those teachings. It is those who proclaim they, or their specific calling, have the truest answers to any and all questions of existing deities and precepts still shrouded in the early imagination of man centuries before. To that leadership I submit the following inquiries.

The question is not where God is or does God exist, even what is God? It's a query proffered in varied forms and in many forums, often within the enclosures of ragged tents in some barren field or from the pulpit ablaze in electronic wizardry, ensconced in a massive, cavernous like structure or the simple church building, alone in a rural area. The intent of the religious speaker is to bring attention to the uncertainty that may still reside in some of his or her congregants. Or the desire to attract a younger generation confused by the battle between technology and traditions of their parents, further assaulted by the cacophony of sound generated by the modern rock music and the increasing and outspoken cadre of youthful celebrities in the entertainment and sports. Such modern day voices tending to mesh into an undefinable dialogue that confuses the unknowing and shocks the unwary. The continuing espousal of opinion and declaration on subjects, most speakers are either too young to understand or too inept in the required knowledge of the subject.

The United States Constitution makes direct reference to freedom of religion and likewise an equal freedom of speech. Others may claim those elements of the First Amendment have not been truly interpreted and remains a vagary of detail as to expansion or limitation. We accept that man is morally responsible and accountable for his or her actions. Just as the eagle does not soar aloft in a vacuum, no man can rise upward to the heights of moral efficacy in an ethical void. Still, within that initial amendment are the agreed rights of those groups who deny the very existence of a God but no assumed rights to deny others of their particular religious viewpoint or assembly.

Many leaders of religious groups, their ministers, priests, pastors, and as designated in some doctrines, their prophet, will contend a personal covenant with God. There, within endless sermons and deigned dialogues lies the speaker's need to affirm its position as a direct conduit with that unknown, invisible and still indistinct God. Whatever the title, the speaker is the protector of the faithful, their provider of moral choices required by their particular faith. Mucilaginous control by the hierarchy of any religious assembly is the power necessary to maintain the structure the domination of its member's free will.

When one considers the variations in any doctrine, they will soon discover that among the more religiously oriented, some will have assured themselves they are destined to the fires of hell, if not sooner, unless they repent. The question arises, what is penance and what form should it take? Is it the litany of prayers issued by the priest in the sanctuary of the confessional or the demand for demonstrations of greater, more stringent expressions of belief required by the more evangelical denominations? An increased degree of physical exertion to demonstrate total devoutness to resolving those admitted transgressions in conflict with the doctrine of that particular religion? Critics of such fervor and faithful obedience to rules and tenets will claim the dedicated adherents give total obeisance to a faceless and formless God. That it is locked in their imagination because they have no other icon to adore. For them, a force, a hope that promises salvation and an inner energy that can and will banish evil in society. Furthermore, that ideological fanaticism prohibits an understanding of practical reality and the natural flaws of mankind.

The Catholic hierarchy cannot sustain any form of democracy. The Pope is the singular leader, without visible dissent or change emanating from any conscious inclusion of differing philosophy and policy. The question arises, are all religions like that? The answer is generally, each have their own manner of ascribing adherence to a particular doctrine or hierarchy and if the hierarchy of that particular belief is just an individual without oversight by a higher authority that religion may be on the verge or has been organized as a cultist accumulation. Catholicism, like most religions, depends on an unwavering attention to its tenets. The Pope cannot allow any reduction in his total and absolute control to become diminished, both within the bishopric hierarchy and especially the word wide congregation of the faithful and their immediate clergy which crosses ethnic, economic and social boundaries.

Control is the critical ingredient in all such undertaking. In the Jewish faith its theology and ancient teachings since the time of Abraham form their religion's hold on its adherents. They may have become more insular over the past centuries with the rising tide of evangelic fervor generated by newer doctrines. Judaism has codified its tenets and rules for personal conduct and relationship with others. It is their heritage they desire to convey to their youth in the face of a modern technology and rush to irrational demands of social media that constantly challenges their traditions and beliefs. The ability of the Jew to resist, yet compromise when required or an advantage, allowed them to bear near untenable misery and surrounding bias as reflected in the Holocaust, the early condemnation by the Catholic church and the ever increasing current wave of anti-Semitism both domestically and abroad.

Followers of Islam pray to Allah as the Jew prays to Yahweh and the Christian to Jesus Christ, unofficially all three a term for an indefinable God. Man may be unable to free himself from the impressions of his youth and the teachings of his parents, a pressure everyone equally faces when young and part of a family that adheres to one theology or another. Those who find the Jewish and Islamic confusing and their differences set in stone need to read the history of both. Each are Semites and have lived together in the same area of the Mideast for centuries. There has arisen in the past hundred years a division within the Islamic faith, engendered by radical elements that has caused harm and violence to other cultures and ethnic identities. It is necessary to bring a degree of light to the shadowy world of what is real and what is portended as fact by those who would misread any disagreement or controversy, be it religion, social and political conflict or their own self-aggrandizement.

We, as the evolution of a particular species, are but a microcosm of what has had' so brief a stay on this planet. To assume we are alone in our ability to control our tomorrows or our position within this spectrum of constant global turmoil, would be at best insipidity. To the religiously bent individual they ascribe some greater influence other than the meek attempts of man to be the final arbiter in discerning the puzzle of life. There are those who would dabble in the arcane practice of mental alchemy by attempting to make godly fervor out of the misapplication of convoluted reasoning. That is their choice, a freedom so cherished.

Man is the curator of his own environment but never consider he is its creator or its owner. However, he is ethically and morally responsible for the custodianship of this wondrous planet. Yet I'm not sure it is to be justified only by more wind turbines or continuous palaver about a climate that has had its way with mankind since the beginning of whatever time period the pundits would declare. As for the much discussed and controversial question of the beginning of the earth, there are many who so strongly contend it was part of the plan of a greater deity. Or as some might offer, it could have just been some God coughing."

"If one reads the Bible or the Koran and later the contended truths supposedly revealed in the writings of the founder of the Church of the Latter Day Saints, Joseph Smith – Mormons, and his successor leader prophets, a common thread is present. In all these documents exists a constant assertion as to the truth being only as they the principal figure have declared it to be or it has been subscribed to in later writings. Now let us point our indicting fingers at this mélange of rules and supposed revelatory testimony encompassed in these religious and doctrinal presentations. Over the last several centuries there has been found increasing information verifying the existence of numerous ancient events and places so much a part of the Torah and the Bible, both Old and New Testament. But in the case of the Koran, as in the case of the Book of Mormon, everything taught that is stated as the history of their particular religion, each doctrine and basic ideology, comes from a single individuals' revelations and personal recollections, according to what is later described in written dictates or interpretation by future supporters, disciples or pupils.

"For Islam, it is the revelations claimed by Mohammed in the seventh century upon which todays self-declared and truly dedicated Muslim devotees base their every actions. Yet it has been shown these reciting's of the voice of Allah have themselves been put in written form only after the death of the original speaker. And this is equally true of the many gospels, reportedly actually written thirty to a hundred years after the reported death of Jesus Christ who was proclaimed the Messiah by his disciples. During the period of early Christendom, even many of those earlier texts, supposedly the basis for the historicity of this new religion, were spurned by the then emerging church hierarchy.

Regrettably, certain verses in the Quran are now mistakenly being assumed as written instructions by the radical segments of that society, to include the constant bloodletting and brutal ravaging so prevalent in Islam's heartland. And is also their constant declaration of being the chosen religion, which I must at this juncture make an aside, is a dogma also propounded by many other theologies. Yet to insist on domination of the world, regardless of the history and devoted adherence of other faiths, has become a bitter diatribe, written in blood on the sands of the Middle East. Regardless, this has been the most incompatible aspects of entire Muslim philosophy. As a cultural entry into mankind's ever evolving progress, they have however, given the world unique architecture, artistic forms and great literary offerings still admired as some of the finest in the history of mankind. Regrettably there has been constant and pitiless attack by associated rogue groups upon a people, the Jews, whose lineage and genealogy not only matches but precedes theirs. A lineage going back to the time of their mutual progenitor Abraham. It is irresponsible that a few uncontrolled individuals within Islam have, by their demand for acceptance through brutality, have created enmity a civilization that brought to the world a period of art and culture rarely duplicated and have soiled the original humanistic chronology of this massive religious movement.

Christianity, although one of the largest of the faith based theologies, has its detractors and is facing a multitude of both ideological and secular problems. The more serious and most publicized, the molestation of youths charges issued against numerous member of the Catholic clergy throughout the world. The Vatican, seat of the entire Catholic world, has appeared far too laggard in its identification and providing local authorities knowledge of these crimes and willingness to allow legal authorities to take charge of the eventual investigation and the punishment.

From the Catholicism of the early church, through its disputes and reformation has arisen numerous similar religious proponents, Protestants, Methodists, Episcopalians, Baptists, Lutherans, of which the number of varied offshoots and sects is endless. They encompass a milieu varying doctrines, always enforcing first, a devotion to the the figure of Jesus and the distinction of being a Christian Christ Perhaps it is necessary that we have the multitude of religions so as to fulfill that myriad of spiritual and moral needs man has craved to answer for millennia." Man is frail in certain aspects of its existence where fear, superstition and lack of knowledge created both inner and assumed physical demons to harass and badger their emotions. But it is those individuals who can psych out the deepest fears in people and determine the weak point in anyone's personal resolve to be free of outside control, who have become the flamboyant and electronically projected celebrities of religious exposition. Providing the bromidic bell adorning the Judas goat leading man to his eventual, intellectual slaughter.

To the critic, these manipulators of searching minds enslave their constituencies into a world where free will and thought are an anathema. Still, membership in such an assembly of like believing and answers seeking compatriots is like being part of their own personal community. In viewing these televised images of thousands of cheering, arms raised and halleluiah shouting individuals being enthused to fill the coffers of self-styled modern day Messiahs, there is the question. Who is the beneficiary and how is the income garnered by new fountains of financial success utilized. Perhaps the personalized ATMs, garbed in religious robes makes it difficult to separate the sincerity of belief in some doctrine from the sound of the cash register behind the pulpit.

The Church of Jesus Christ of Latter Day Saints, the LDS or Mormons, as better known, became the dual epitome of certain religious odysseys in their one hundred eighty five year history. Its beginning, a mixture of historical fact and disputed actions of a young man in in the rural area of upstate New York. Tales, claimed by its early members and part of the doxology of the church as factual happenings. The visitation to a youth, a Joseph Smith by heavenly figures representing the supreme deity, the unearthing upon request by the visitors of golden plates from which the later Book of Mormon was ostensibly written.

An individual known in his youth as a constant treasure seeker and believer in the folk legend inspired mysticism at the time. Along with others in his area who felt assured magic was an element of many events seeming strange or unexplainable during the early 19th Century where he lived. From there, creation of a church based on those writings, the propagation of membership then in the midst of roving evangelical outings and declared prophets of every nature and belief. Eventually, formation of an ever growing membership using new members eager to spread the word through missionary travels to such places as England and other northern domiciles.

From that basic organization, Smith and his followers moved several times to other sites considered more acceptable to his new doctrine. As often with new concepts or beliefs, the enmity of other people not in favor of Smith's especial brand of biblical interpretation rose and created harsh environs for the new converts to Smith's teachings. Later he and several others were arrested in Nauvoo, IL and slain by a dissenting mob of locals. To be fair to the members of what has become one of the largest religious configurations in the world, it would be better for those interested in the fascinating history of the Mormons to take the time to read of their early beginnings, the hardships and prejudice they have suffered over the years. It would take far too much print here to appropriately encompass the story of that unique entry into the faiths of the world. Smith was to his early followers a prophet as is the title of each succeeding leaders of the church.

An important part of the LDS is its vaunted missionary program that makes the Jehovah's Witness solicitation program look like a temporary employee system. Yet to send near pubescent youths out into a dangerous world fraught with trial and tribulation is at best a tenuous manner of proselyting. At age eighteen to twenty, the LDS youth is just approaching the doorstep of adulthood. To position them possibly in harm's way without the experience normally required is to propagate the faith by presupposing some type of divine protection which is not always the case. The hierarchy of the LDS do utilize an almost total control of local government and social conduct in their home state of Utah.

The president of the LDS, at the spring, 2021 'General Conference' emanating from Salt Lake City, announced an addition 20 temples to be constructed. Of that number are to be built in foreign countries. Interestingly one will be located in Cali Columbia, home of one of the largest, most violent drug cartels in South America. Another in Singapore which is under Chinese domination and another in the African nation whose poverty level has decimated the population there for years. The church currently has over 250 operating temples in the United States and throughout the world, or those under construction or will soon begin construction.

There is a question asked by many. Who pays for these structures? They are large, architecturally designed in a similar style and used rarely, mostly for baptisms, special ceremonies and weddings. That last occasion can occur only if the couple are members in good standing of the church, meaning compliance with the conditions of membership. Oddly enough, unless guests, including immediate family also have the required documentation of faithful tithing and adherence to the prescribed fellowship. For those unaware of the term 'tithing', it is the Mormon title for the ongoing contribution to the church. It is reported the normal compliance is ten percent of an individual's yearly income, but that is ostensibly subject to the discretion of the church itself.

Too many people concentrate on the Mormon's previous acceptance of polygamy in its beginning years until the desire and requirement for statehood brought an official revelation assumedly ending the practice. To date the multitude of LDS congregants believe polygamy is now a part of their past. Still, there exist a few smaller groups bunches of disaffected older individuals living out in the more deserted part of the west and several locations in Canada and elsewhere who still pursue polygamy as a required aspect of their revised Mormon ideology. This writer would suggest this is merely a method for these avowed revised LDS doxology advocates to allow a group of males to very young females and violating the law just to get into the panties of underage girls. If one wishes a view of a more sophisticated and lesser noticed polygamy, go to Hollywood or the SoHo in New York, or wherever you have large concentrations of self-endowed free spirits. Those people have been indiscriminatingly bedroom hopping for years, producing more children without defined or caring parent than can be measured.

Mormonism has been the focus of attempted validation of their every belief and equally, criticism of many of their purported doctrines and historical past and actions of their leadership. An interesting comment was part of the introduction to the autobiography of John D. Lee, published in 1877. Lee, a devout member of the Mormons, was the sole convicted participant in the infamous "Mountain Meadow Massacre", Sept. 11, 1857, of an immigrant wagon train which occurred in southern Utah, perpetrated by a group of Mormon militants and a number of southern Piute Indians. In Lee's book, "Mormonism Unveiled", he accused the then leader/prophet of the church, Brigham Young of either ordering or knowing ahead of the event that an attack would take place. Lee's attorney, Wm. W. Bishop wrote in the preface, "Mormonism is in part a conglomeration of ill cemented credos from other religions ..." Rebuffed and condemned by church hierarchy, it still became one of the more shocking exposes of a religious group already under criticism by other faiths.

Judgement by their peers and probable required reinstallation of the basic tenets and rules of the particular faith are required when it has been decided by the religious leadership some nature of violation has occurred. In some religions, excommunication is possible. In others, dissolution from the church's congregation and in several lesser known followings, "shunning" or personal and social isolation of the member found guilty of lack of total obeisance to the rules of the group. Unfortunately for those of the Islamic faith, final resolution of any such accusations or offenses can lead to more serious penalties not necessary to mention here. To those in control of any such group, nonconformity is apostasy or heresy – marking disloyalty. To the nonbeliever or the agnostic, it is instead merely free thought and free will expression.

In the area of the more bizarre doctrinal convictions is the Hollywood clique that so fervently proclaim their devotion to Scientology. For a group who also favor unattached physical meanderings and producing children of mysterious origin as well as keeping the drug market and the psychiatric rehabilitation industry well supported, Scientology has become the chic spiritual undertaking. To its critics, the former space novel author and new fad theology founder Ron L. Hubbard, he found many eager candidates within the movie and music industry folds. To observers, the principle aspect of Scientology is the insistence on expensive doctrinal training, written materials and special seminars to both enthuse and reconstitute the member's allegiance – normally requiring additional financial contribution by the member. My opinion of Scientology as a religion is somewhat biased as I recognize its operational format and intense emphasis is primarily on total loyalty to the organization and the ability to pay to pray.

Whether it is the media, radical voices on both sides and incompetent campaign advisors, there is a disconcerting emphasis on a political candidate's personal religious history. Something in a system of governance wherein the state and religion are supposedly marked as separated and such division inviolable under the constitution. Insertion of the religious history of any candidate is of little relevance and does a disservice to the electoral process. It obfuscates the relationship between the agreed rights of both the church and the state. Whether Barack Obama was affected by the fiery rhetoric of the anti-Semite, Rev. Jeremiah Wright, or was an adherent of the Koran or his supporters influenced to refute the religion of his presidential opponent, a recognized Mormon, is of no legitimate value. It tramples on the freedoms of choice we supposedly respect so much.

But such conjectures retain their substance to fall within future meat for discussion by those who enjoy such past soirees in *what ifs*. Such considerations could become salient if he or she, after assuming the Oval Office, would expect everyone to join in dancing around a decorated holiday tree at every pagan solstice, sans any form of clothing. Then there might be a bit of backlash from the other religions. Leashing a candidate to his or her religion is not the critical question when entering the voting booth, it is which individual offers the most probable and viable choice to achieve what we as individuals wish to see accomplished. Then we can either go to a church of our choice or just head for the golf course or a late breakfast. That is the decision of a free person in this country, a freedom that must be preserved – regardless of any electoral outcome.

For the absolute cynic, the totally mismanaged and reticence of the Vatican to fully investigate and take immediate action involving the constant reports of youth molestation and inappropriate actions by numerous clergy will be its millstone around the neck of the current and possibly future pontiffs. The Islamic faith has also suffered accusations of innate evil, never substantiated or proven in any manner. The Jewish faith continues to suffer anti-Semitism, increasing in several parts of the world, embarrassingly even in the United States. Their legacy of suffering remains once of mankind's most conscious prejudices. The LDS has been accused of cult like similarity to other more drastically exaggerated religious pronouncements which seem to have no basis. The celebrity laden, financial version of a Ponzi scheme, the Church of Scientology in Hollywood will continue as the celebrity dilettantes remain avid believers and fiscal supporters.

The world of religious fervor has been seriously marked in the minds of many by the earlier rantings of Jim Jones whose false dogma caused the deaths of over 900 innocent people in the jungles of Guinea French Guiana. Or the infamous Dr. Doe or David Koresh whose idiotic theocracy and ideology also caused the death of many innocents by diluted religious adherents regrettably aided by possibly an inadequate assault process by federal law enforcement. The Church of Jesus Christ of Latter Day Saints has moved more away from that vague earlier precepts engendered by its founder regarding certain aspects of mysticism and magic. It joined into the wider general public of religious offerings. This included the acceptance of blacks into the church's priesthood, an increased but still minimal acceptance of female equality and eventual recognition of `same sex marriage' and the rising influence of the LGBT populace.

Our younger generation is uncomfortable as they face the enormous body of established facts which have been proven and claimed by such sciences as astronomy, chemistry, biology, physics, anthropology and others have provided. We have come to understand that man is haunted by the problem of knowledge. If the increasing discoveries of the natural sciences foster agnosticism then where is the more religiously oriented to go to find the truth of their personal existence? These opposing and confusing positions encouraged doubt by our youths about their particular religious faith or ideology. Or is such is even of need or importance what with the rise of new Gods proposed by the celebrity prophets of the entertainment, sports and technology scenes.

As the technology of information grows exponentially, more and more new theories or concepts on personal freedoms and need for individual agendas proliferate the youth of today. Celebrity advocates become the newest prophets of what should be the role of the younger generation, their rights and demand for an equality that many see as a danger to what is determined the traditional social order. Voices from the world of modern music and the glamour of Hollywood and tabloid personalities can quickly disturb the parent/child relationship. During these times of social confusion and dissonant challengers of what was, the pressure on parents and associated caretakers in the educational and law enforcement area will continue.

Conforming to theories taught by their parents, sometimes rigorously inculcated during their early years, the youth of every generation will feel restricted, too bound by the warnings of those outside the parental enclosure. Friends, associates, educational overseers to have the greater influence on the thinking of our children. The study of the human mind reveals limitations of thought and in the younger years it is merely an observation of a growing phenomenon, the development of the immature into what ostensibly is to be an adult cognizance. But the examination of the mentality of lower animals also promotes the theorem by some that man is only a superior thinking animal. And as such, man being the only specie with the proven ability to think reasonably, it is further noted to be the only specie to be unreasonable.

For those who may feel I have impugned the place of religion within our social structure, you are mistaken. My intent was not to challenge or negate any beliefs or the organized structures and administration of any of these particular theologies. I fully support the right of anyone seeking their personal emotional and psychological relief in the varied forms of the "balm of Gilead" whatever the form it takes. Rather, my goal was to briefly survey both the strengths and existing fragilities of religion in both their actual organization and that which most markedly forms the criticism of their rivals or antagonists.

As to religions' various involvements, especially in the world of political candidacy and other secular subjects outside their purview, I quote from Irish dramatist, Sean O'Casey's "The Plough and the Stars," as follows. "There's no reason to bring religion into it. I think we ought to have as great a regard for religion as we can, so as to keep it out of as many things as possible."

Chapter 12

Whispering Against the Wind

The 2020 political campaign was laden with promises, plans and the normal threats uttered when the opposition had posed a policy or intent, upon victory, to emplace *some dastardly plan* to destroy or alter another American tradition. Forgiving those with lofty ideals and subsequent plans to improve what they feel is broken and the often hasty rebuttal by opponents, now is a time for the writer to submit those personal concerns presented by the litany of needed change and steadfast resistance that is so much a part of the political polemic panoply. Bear with the writer as the following issues have been mentioned earlier in brief or more cogent to the subject being discussed. Still, they remain bones of contention and will shadow upcoming national and state legislatures and administrators for years to come. They will not merely disappear but will remain the conscious attention of voters until resolved.

Several of the early Democrat nominee aspirants were quite vocal about eliminating current college student debt. Others modified their agreement in the terms of a lower amount of reduction or an altering the interest level served on such debts. Access to education is a right for all citizens and those with valid entry documents to this country. As for the undocumented, that is a variance that has to be considered in another discussion. It falls between human rights and opportunities granted the eligible. We leave that caveat to the more authorized to deal with. Yet, were such laws and debt cancellation procedures to be enacted, freeing many heretofore economically pressured students and/or their parents, what of the result? Who then compensates the colleges, community colleges and universities for the loss of the revenue that supports the many aspects of collegian experience? Are there avenues of approach regarding initial funding of tuition and other specific factors, books, on campus housing coupled with temporary work opportunities?

That all having been resolved who then is responsible for all those lost funds provided either through government grants and loans, or the banks through whom the parents and occasional students were able to transact such lending? Undoubtedly quite pleasing to the more advanced liberal consideration, were the demand for basically free or much reduced costs for higher education succeeds in being implemented, who determines how such fiscal advantage is to be bestowed? To whom, under what conditions and to what extent of projected individual expenses is this benefit allowed? Is this to become an additional entitlement and where does it fit within an already rapidly expanding national debt? In addition, how constitutionally viable is the removal of such indebtedness to the lending institutions? Response to these questions would make for a fascinating series of public debates. Definitely ample fodder for prime time talk shows or special television presentations.

Apparently the continuing issue of increased educational costs were over looked or purposely omitted during the raucous political debate commentary. Tuitions rising, added fees for services and special amenities once thought necessary for the normal college experience. The addition of staff without cost accounting. The extension of that time away from classroom instruction obligations for those who have reached academic tenure and are allowed paid leave to seek research for writing their next dissertations that also engenders their income and magnify their cognoscenti' prestige. Their absence in that same classroom replaced by assistant instructors or other less experienced and erudite resource.

Next we come to the ongoing demands for law enforcement reform. The immediate cries to defund local police operations or completely eliminating their basic services as bizarre and insensible knee jerk reactions and beyond reason. Thus, the question is when are the local, state and national groups to be involved going to begin this effort? Who should comprise such committees? What should be the legislatively granted authority for such groups to actually have their recommendations and procedural decisions placed into effect and to be monitored henceforth as to ability and consistency of implementation under ongoing review?

Without the appropriate and substantive law giving such bodies the authority to call witnesses, experts, prepared agendas and later policy guidelines, it will become an exercise in futility. Furthermore, to acquire, train and solidify the right of supervising commanders and municipal officials the authority to provide the oversight and correction of any and all future prohibited actions such as generated the past misdeeds bringing about this quandary. There will always exist the increased costs, a sensitive subject for local officials attempting to pacify the needy while limiting excessive tax burden to others. Already too many cities have been drawing unceasingly from the well of taxable input only to find the well may be drying up, sooner than ever expected.

The psychology of the street encounter, the the reevaluated extent of physical and procedural training are critical. The response to community cultural sensitivities are an elemental part of any changes. This along with the cooperation of minority leadership in being diligent in both partaking in these policy reviews and demanding their minority constituents understand the efforts being attempted. The use of trained social workers can be part of the process but remembering unarmed individuals cannot be unduly exposed to situations such as domestic violence or abuse that can, and too often does require forceful intervention. Fear comes from the unknown, reaction is often in support of a lack of awareness or experience. The potential police officer candidate must be adjudged as much by his or her psychological profile as to the physical size, educational level and conversational skills. We cannot create the motion picture version of *"Robocop"*, but rather public representatives with the skill and temperament to be a vital part of the community they serve. And as mentioned before, such improvement costs. Still not as deleterious to a community as violent protests, litigation and the stain of disgraced police officers.

The ensuing protests as referred to earlier, are protected by the first Amendment, one of the freedoms unique to our country but sadly abused at times. Rules that protect collateral citizen attendance from purposeful attack or threatened harm must be considered illegal and immediately prosecuted. Such allowance is not reflected within the First Amendment wording. The use of bullhorns, screaming obscenities, noise creation and trespassing on private property to annoy and harass protest targets late at night and without cessation is also a violation of those individual's rights and must suffer the same penalties as other similar illegal acts. If the move by some legislative jurisdictions to decriminalize any riot related crimes generated by the current mode of protests, would create a new category of legal interpretation. What had been evident violations of the law, using the current standards, would now be invalidated as to punishment under the cloak of being a justified part of violence during any protest engagement. That said, to do violence against another does nothing and be immune from prosecution, disgraces the principle of the rule of law and ennobles the wrongdoer.

It is imperative with the aging of society itself and the growing need of the lesser advantage we discuss medical care But to what extent and for whom? Truly one of the most troubling situations in our country today is the lack of sufficient medical care for those who have limited economic stature, are part of the increasing homeless population or who are finding increasing medical expense for they and their families and is burying them in financial frustration. The cost of pharmaceuticals need continued and effective oversight by the appropriate government agency. The rising cost of prescription medicines, countered by the major suppliers as being the cost of developing newer and more effective drugs has to be documented by an agency equipped to equate research costs with eventual consumer pricing.

The entire inability to meet the growing health needs of both the indigent and the elderly population is a conundrum this writer is ill-equipped to offer any substantive suggestions. Still, it must be addressed by those in power and effective measures developed, and now. The homeless, for whom each tomorrow may be their last, must be categorized as to need, hopefully a degree of support and importantly, a greater insight as to how each of them entered this darkening time of their lives. Proposed "single payer plans", part of the early campaign oratory still face a detailed explanation as to possible process and – of course – what the cost will be and who will pay that cost. "Obama Care" was touted as the cure all for the previously mentioned inadequacies. It became an administrative and fiscal nightmare causing even greater economic burden both on the government mandated system and those who enrolled.

The immigration issue will be part of our national dilemma so long as we remain the doorkeeper to the one general social order and governmental system looked to by a large part of the globe's inhabitants as offering a freedom and opportunity unknown or disallowed in many countries. At the base of the Statue of Liberty, a gift of the French people, is the simple quote, "Give me your tired, your poor, your huddled masses yearning to be free . . ." Sincerely meant but over the years with the influx of many undesirable, criminally intended individuals flowing to our borders within the masses of earnest applicants for entry, the problem increases daily. The need for vetting is at best complex and appearing impossible to correct. Yet, it must be addressed an orderly manner including to what degree do those allowed entry have to stipulate their desire to become a citizen or are just taking refuge from worsening conditions from where they have come. And when admitted, to what extent are these different groups to be granted the benefits expected and provided citizens already here?

The opposition to the "immigrant" issue and for a more politically correct phraseology, the "undocumented", will always continue as long as fear of personal position and diminishment of opportunity that exists for those already enjoying the benefits of our nation. At the moment of writing this particular section, the new President Biden has announced that within one hundred days of his inauguration, he would send a bill to the Senate requesting citizenship for several million undocumented individuals now in this country. If passed and becomes a *fait accompli,* it would provide many additional tax supported benefits for these fortunate individuals and assure the Democratic Party a measurably increased voter edge in certain parts of the country for local, state and national elections.

Like many aspects of the political world, it remains just a numbers game. As this book was being completed, he'd already directed the reentry of several thousand individuals previously deported during the Trump administration. Coupled with that, in one of his immediate post inauguration flurry of Executive orders, he directed the border wall then under construction, halted, leaving a portion of that border without any form or resistance to the flow of undocumented individuals from Central America. Additionally, access restrictions would be measurably lowered and the vetting process greatly reduced.

The Electoral College has again popped its controversial head above the absence of consideration over the past four years. Only since the defeat of Hillary Rodham Clinton who amassed a three million popular vote total over her opponent in 2026 has the cry to move to the one person, one vote once more come to the fore. In the case of the recent election however, the massive greater popular vote has again convinced the supporters of the need to eliminate the electoral vote. As referred to earlier, it becomes a numbers game with little concern by its advocates of the smaller populated areas of the country and the assured domination of the presidency by less than a dozen larger urban complexes. Even with the burgeoning move to eliminate that form of final candidate selection, the fact remains that the current resident of 1600 Pennsylvania Ave. and the members of Congress who faced close elections in 2020 will for the next four years face over seventy four million voters for whom the present administration was not their choice.

Gun control in any form has become the rally cry of those using the various killing of innocent peoples in groups by use of what are commonly referred to as assault weapons. To the obverse, it is equally the vehement denial of any such controls by those who feel this would literally abolish the 2nd Amendment. Those who would desire the drastic elimination of most weapons ownership, their contention that the at the time of the amendment's writing, weapons were muzzle loading, on potential shot ability perhaps two a minute at most. Today, they chorus the concerns of those who fear the increase in multi cartridge loaded, extremely rapid firing rifles of numerous types and capabilities. It will be a veritable bramble bush of contradictory suggestions and opinions as to what degree such controls might be implemented and the litigation soon to follow. Once more dear reader, I leave that walk through the minefield of dissident dialogue to others far more astute than I.

We now approach a subject of great interest to every parent. Access to sufficient education has long been the desire pf parents for their children, the agreed opening in the doorway to greater opportunity and the benefits of gainful employment and both higher social and economic plateaus. The debate still rages as to whether the states and local school administrations should remain the primary determiner of policy and continue its control of all related matters in the education of the children in their individual jurisdictions. Or can and should the national government take charge, creating a master control, developing and dictating the prescribed needs and operation of all elementary, middle and high schools in the United States and its territories.

With the ongoing threat of litigation, school board decisions or actions by individual school officials force many local school administrators to be inactively frozen with the inability to properly carry out their assigned function. They understandably fear immediate censure by higher authorities and the always present shadow of the ACLU, prepared to take any dispute or parent and student objections to court. To the supporters of a major change it would clarify and standardize what is often a cacophony of voices demanding resolution of disagreement to their personal favor. To those who object to further intrusion into matters primarily the concern and responsibility of local and state officials, it is an attempt to allow government excessive control in conflict with the intentions of the Constitution.

In this related dichotomy also exists the institution and at times almost totalitarian administration of rules specifying certain conduct, prohibiting other actions and using suspension and expulsion without appropriate hearing or semblance of reasonable review. Too many school administrators have assumed title of authority and commanding interference in situation that may have resulted from their own unreasoned abuse of their position to earn public or political acceptance. And in the field of higher education, the seemingly roughshod need to assuage the complaints or denials of certain groups have eliminated many conservative speakers from campuses. Forced various pseudo equality based academic courses on incoming freshman and fallen prey to instantaneous and irresponsible reaction to claims of disparity of races and social classes.

The rise in greater legal substance to particular complaints or objections to specific rules or procedures has invested the pre adult age group with far more legal standing than ever previously imagined. Agreed, the student is the primary object of operational efficiency and effort. Yet, there must be an equal degree of acceptance that the adult mind and supervisory structure has to have the modicum of control and right to pursue reasonable curricula of action and policy that will assures a sense of agreeable position of authority. Without a measured level of responsible academic and operational structure we have only dissonance without culpability or resolution.

As part of recitation of the most publicized future options, once more we include the disgusting misuse and constant abuse of the expressions, race, racial and racism. Parleyed to an insufferable degree for political advantage and social recrimination, once again, race as a word is generally accepted as "a category of humankind that shares certain distinctive physical traits." The exponents of racial equality are subject to hyper activism in using these expressions to often hide their own personal agenda which when revealed has more to do with acquisition of power over a particular situation or objective than the actual desire for equality. It is very evident and we must accept that many of us are insensitive to racial inclusion in various aspects of employment, social status and legal parity.

Attempts to designate a white culture specie as violating the rights of all others is in itself to deter logical and reasoned discussion of racial divides that do and regrettably may exist into the future. Our children and those entering colleges are now faced with mandatory courses in how to demean the supposed white culture while accepting shame for being part of that same assembly. It is a human flaw that although possible to lessen, hopefully to cleanse from many activities and judgements but in reality can never be fully erased. It has been with us since the emergence of the earliest human genre. Its diminishment will take coordinated effort, sans the efforts by some to utilize this unsuitable division to their personal advantage. Allegorically, when you ride that tiger of superiority over all others, the ride is adrenalin achieving and inwardly fulfilling. Yet, the true danger is when you dismount the tiger.

Chapter 13

The Newest Venal Expression

Race, racism, racial, expressions used today as cudgels to subject those considered offending the current rule, to alter existing tradition and to instill fear in those who would have opinion in conflict with those in power.

Let's examine this four letter abomination of misused language. Here is a definition from the depths of academia on the subject of human evolution. Race – an identifiable group of people who share common descent – coming originally from the Greek, word, "genus." Basically a combination of the expression "genos", referring to race or kind and "gonos", which meant related to birth, offspring, common qualities, origin and familial stock. We are told there are three basic races, Caucasoid, Mongoloid and Negroid. Enough of the detail and explanation merely transcribed from current scientific babble. Now, an alternate definition of how the expression may have come into being.

Millennials ago, when mankind had finally risen from the mire of prehistoric slime, according the the evolutionists, there was no racial disparity. What occurred was the immediate notice by one individual or group or tribe of humans that another similar species was different in some manner. Size, weight, facial or body configuration, who really knows. Rather than from the beginning, there was no homogenous gathering of humanoids into a singular specie or configuration, accepted by all who encountered one another. From the Neanderthal through the developing Cro-Magnon, considered the stereotype for today's modern man, the noted variations were not racial – but by our ancestors, considered differences.

The early African species, some eventually journeying northward and then onward to other diverse part of the globe. And if one is to accept all the precepts from Darwin to the recognized anthropologists, paleontologist and ethnologists, the multitude of cultures, physical structures to survive in whatever climate they evolved, and their definitive appearances, became the society of mankind we know today. The continual reference to past subjugations of various groups of people, the Jews of the age of Pharaohs, the native residents of Africa, and onto the more recent rejection of incoming Slavic, middle European, Asian and Irish immigrants entering this country in early 19th to early 20th Century.

The Jewish people were not enslaved by the Pharaohs because of their race. They'd been captured by the Babylonians, late finding themselves in the Egyptian Empire. And when the need for cheap labor arose for continuation of the massive construction projects, the "odd" religious beliefs of the Hebrews, made them prime candidates for slavery. That's not racial, is it? If so than, banning a drunk from your bar, perhaps or a teacher dismissing a student from the classroom for sleeping during the instruction? Or a business refusing to prepare a wedding cake for two men or two women planning to marry each other? Or would some contend, yes that's discrimination and that has a racial context. Now we're collecting various reasons for one person not wishing to associate or provide service to another person to be identified as a racists.

Perhaps we need a new law stating that any discriminating selection process, refusal to accept another person's request, to deny participation of anyone in a gathering as automatic racism is now racists. Forget the other expressions. We need to be rid of the various government departments handling the different charges of unfairness. Just a czar of racial equality judgement. Could save a few tax dollars – I assume. The question of how to define and thus, to deal with such a plethora of various actions into one word – race – would be a semantic Rubric Cube for those who deal with the English language as a profession.

The history of one more powerful entity controlling a less endowed population through conflict, the vicissitudes of nature, draught, pestilence, is legendary. To the conqueror, the subjected peoples weren't necessarily chosen because of enmity toward whatever ethnic background. They were looked on as spoils of war or conflict, as property, to be utilized as felt needed or desired. Unfortunately the black man, principally the African born or those of the dark skin indicating ethnic affiliation with the black man, became primary the primary source of slaves among many nations, empires, kingdoms. It is not this writer's contention that at any time during man's unfolding development, slavery was ever morally acceptable, other than it being the opinion of human worth at that time.

Unfortunately, the new world of what would become the United States, Central and South America, became the site of vast enslavement, the indigenous Indian population in those areas and the needs of a developing agrarian culture in the pre-colonial days of our nation. That tragic episode of our country's emergence has been discussed by many others so I leave further elucidation on the subject to them. The Civil war of 1860-65, saw the supposed end to slavery. The intent of the then current president Abraham Lincoln was to institute systems and programs to allow the former slaves to enter society on and equal and fulfilling basis. However, with the assassination of Lincoln, the accession to the presidency by Andrew Johnson, the Democratic candidate originally emplaced to assist acquiring need cotes, the hopes of the black man were dashed. Johnson acceded control of any attempt at reconstruction to the still Democratic dominated southern legislative, judicial and law enforcement systems. For the next one hundred years, domination, legally, legislatively, economically and socially impressed the black communities into a veritable revalidation of their days in bondage.

It was here that race, the ever present chains that bound the black man to impoverishment, lack of opportunity and constant personal fear, became the working mantra of the white establishment. To avoid the clear identity of the inequality, the black person was subjected to the claims of inferior levels of cognizant reasoning, an aptitude for theft and falsity and particularly, a natural tendency to be laggard in any assigned job or function. When the fulcrum of public attitude began to swing away from the southern posture, it was the national legislature and succeeding residents of the White house who either avoided interference in the then status quo or were contributor to the unspoken racial discrimination, a part of the south similarly practiced in the northern climes although well hidden by those not desiring the possible public wrath.

The use of race as a deterrent to societal evolution has become the accepted doctrine to some, unfortunately still a part of numerous legislative, local administrations and law enforcement attitudes leading to oppressive practices by all concerned. As we began to demonstrate true understanding to the discriminatory nature of certain organizations and operations, race, and its semantic use became one of the most effective tools of the politician, the legislator, the candidate to elected office. Furthermore, it became the buzzword, the headline maker for the media who joined with the political coterie to use the word as a preamble to many reportable situations having no relationship to race as a factor.

Sadly, the abominable institution that Abraham Lincoln ostensibly abolished with the Emancipation Proclamation Act. Is becoming resurgent to the degree that the new slavery is to conformity. George Orwell spoke of it in his volumes,   "1984," and "Animal Farm." The bondage is represented by the attempted control of speech which when considered in conflict with the newly adjust norm, must be squelched or at least modified to fit the required template. Racism has become too integrated into the language of legal preparation. It permeates the think of those preparing accusations or defining defensive tactics. The word's misuse can easily cause confusion which allows emotion to take precedence. Dominating the basic question of wrong or right of an accusation, a charge or complaint, law must never put form over substance and fact.

It is difficult to muzzle those who use words in a context only to either rationalize their distorted thinking or to accelerate an existing situation to fit their personal agenda. They will, and in the case of several of the most publicized "white privilege" and "systemic racism" revilers, have exacerbated recent situations involving black citizen/police officer encounters that tragically resulted in a death. Such prostitution of polemics will never be lessened until these architects of public distress are called to account by their celebrity colleagues. It's not understood why such manipulators of the media and other legislators have this influence. Unless it is fear by others that they too will become the target of these career carnival hucksters unless they show obeisance to their demagoguery.

Chapter 14

An Epilogue, Ever Changing

There is the common feeling in many areas that the world is in midst of a major and possibly climatic epic of human history. A current opinion, mankind is experiencing a social and moral revolution, unparalleled in scope and intensity. Unrest and turmoil throughout the globe affects all people, their institutions and particularly their religious and political ideologies. Is it possible that man is entangled in a vast and complex web which he himself cleverly designed and boldly spun without conscious recognition? No man or nation can become genuinely great without dedication to those principles that undergird their ethical values. Integrity of the civilization so often depends upon sound ideas but it must be safeguarded by honest and honorable administrators.

During the 20th century, as the pace of human affairs enormously accelerated through the massively expanding technology, it should be much easier to observe the conditions that are both helpful and harmful to our potential as a productive and freedom protecting nation. Within the last one hundred years, wars and blood purges and tyrannical genocides have cost multiple millions of human lives. We have come to accept that the aftermath of wars and vicious internal discords are usually more degenerative socially and morally than was the military conflict itself. Scientific knowledge is now so imposing that a host of people have become agnostic about supernatural reality. That of course is their freedom of expression while one must assume there will always be those who believe solidly and fully in the religious value of our society than merely the pure applications of any field of science or social conduct.

Throughout the world, struggle for material resources and particularly political power and independence is growingly severe. To generalize, the demand for security and progress by its people merely exacerbates the lust for power by those they have chosen or have been forced to bear as administrators. Caution is needed with the advent of greater reliance on governmental paternalism as it increases. Under the specious assumption that centralized governmental care and control introduces a utopian society, it allows people to become increasingly disposed to delegate their personal initiatives and responsibilities to national agencies. Thus they soon incur the potentially serious risk of abuse of personal freedom.

Good government is the crux of any nation or civilization's survival. It's a means of protecting inalienable rights of people. It should respect and adhere to principles that under gird personal worth and supporting free man's hopes for opportunity and accessibility. Without good government, wisely administered, a democracy can't survive. It is what binds the best interests of those being governed with the ethical mandate that should hopefully control all such administrative, economic, judicial and political actions of those legitimately selected to lead via vote of the citizenry. However when people surrender their sacred to rights to a centralized bureaucracy, they are encouraging the rise of dictatorial forces that inevitably will reduce them to the status of human pawns and puppets. 2500 years ago Plato and later the writer Lord Acton and others stated that those in positions of power usually develop a greater craving for power. Compressing their thoughts, "power corrupts and absolute power corrupts absolutely".

The national ambition for social and economic progress and the increasing demand for support of science and technology encourages the federal government to allocate billions of dollars annually in support of education. However, where that money is spent and how effective its administration has become a matter of great suspicion and disappointing revelations of inadequacy and blatant incompetence. Too many secular education institutions rely too strongly on the national treasury for substantial financial support. In this manner they, at least implicitly, yield to governmental authority for guidance. It appears that many administrators of sectarian educational institutions do not understand how such increased government subsidy or financial support may lead to mollifying or modifying the objectives and policies of education. It's a most challenging effect, the insufficiency of quality and substantive educational opportunities for our children – those in whose hands will lie the administration and protection of this nation for generations to come.

We understand that freedom of thought and religion and freedom of worship are sacred trusts which must be safeguarded as it has been over the last two plus centuries with the blood and sacrifice of many Americans. To be free, people must stand resolutely upon the foundation of enduring truth and ethics and this precious human freedom cannot be evaluated primarily in terms of material wealth, social security and political prowess. The inferior actions by inferior government officials, including legislatures, do not promote respect for the truth. The resolute mind of humanity is achieved by means of great ideas and constant devotion to those principles that first engendered the concept of individual liberty and freedom of expression. You cannot buy wisdom at a bargain counter nor purchase a ticket of admission to the exalted levels of the very successful. A country may become efficient and powerful under a dictatorship or forced obeisance for a short time while but soon its citizens will realize they are slaves and freedom will again cost personal sacrifice and potentially lives as it did in the early days of our founding.

We must understand that man is morally responsible and accountable for his or her actions. Just as an eagle does not soar aloft in a vacuum no man can rise to the heights of moral efficacy in an ethical vacuum. Our world is an exciting drama, the plot is human destiny and mankind is the principal actor on the stage. We are constantly faced with an ever-increasing series of actions, many of which are totally outside the realm of reason. One action will arouse optimism, yet another lacking moral judgement and conscious recognition of the potential evil it may garner, will create depression. Asking mankind whether they should rely upon nature seems to be at best a question totally devoid of reality. We are an integral part of the society we have developed over the millennia since mankind's first appearance on this planet. True, we are commanders of our destiny and have control of a technology never before so advanced. Yet we are still constantly subject to the laws of nature.

It is a known fact of life that however productive nature may be, she promises death to every creature to which she gives birth. And this makes no exception for man. Nature makes no answer from a grave nor will it speak a word of hope for the many cemeteries or unknown internments to which some feel mankind will eventually consign all living creatures. We progressed from primitive barbarism to modern civilization as a result of the ways we have learned to use our ability and initiative. But does science and technology supply man's basic needs and satisfy his ultimate concern? However useful and well filled our warehouses with material gadgetry, can man live and find both physical and emotional security and hope in them alone? As refers to the institution of governments, man relies upon government. Duly constituted government is essential to an efficient and freely functioning civilization. If government seems to step over that line of demarcations that protects human and civil rights, rather than taking up arms it should occur at the voting booth and not in violent protest on the streets.

Yet, however large, wealthy or powerful any nation becomes it will eventually decline unless constantly bolstered by the demand for ethical and moral behavior coupled with conscious attention to the needs of its citizenry. History offers numerous examples regarding the failure of a people following the weakening of their guarantee of individual freedoms but still gives us no final answer to how such situations can be reversed. The shame of those espousing the a rush to rewrite history through immediate destruction of memorials or symbols that marked past events or participants just to meet current beliefs or ideological interpretation is to destroy the lessons on which our younger generation begins the learning process. The difficulty lies in the fact that such radicalism fails to note that history will just keep happening regardless of our efforts to interpret or understand its moving pattern.

In the span of religious influence, both ancient and modern, we find beliefs and practices of almost every conceivable type, quality and quantity. They often raise sheer superstition to levels of accepted reverence and unfeigned adoration of whatever God has been designed as the Supreme Being. Political ambition and religious intolerance, not infrequently combined, have produced enormous concern for the ages. There is no other odor as offensive as that of piety tainted with evil as is so often reflected in political dialogue. Moreover, the use of religion for personal purposes to support near Machiavellian political objectives and to enhance personal secular interests merely brings closer that end to those freedoms critical to this nation's survival. To those who are strongly and avidly of religious mind, its beliefs becomes dogmatic and intolerant, they are required to constantly consider the values and needs expressed by others who may not be of their faith. For those who give credence to deism or others who declare God as such does not exist and we are the product of certain natural confluences, their rights as protected by the constitution must faithfully observed and protected.

Although man has gained dominion over many things both nature and he created, he finds himself dealing constantly with` amazing successes and desultory failure. We are exploring the physical universe but what of the ethical and moral conduct being required of him or her who have been selected to lead specific groups or constituencies. Both religious and secular literature abounds with examples of foolish blunders. In Shakespearean literature, Macbeth, notably a man of unusual stature, allowed selfish motives to dominate his ambition and caused his death. Actually dying morally before the time he was killed. Today the peccadilloes of the political, entertainment and sports celebrities, hidden by an unknowing or complicit media but eventually revealed, are primary fodder in today's food market tabloids.

The manner in which our national and in many cases our national and state legislatures attempt to gain mastery over matters traditional within the private domain creates a distrust of their every administrative move. Today we face a situation in a national administration where chosen leaders are hypnotically fascinated by their own supposed accomplishments. They overlook the essential nature of the free mind and display a blatant disregard for the truth of reality. The deliberate action of our national legislators, the Executive branch and even the suspect approaches of our judiciary has caused an aura of mistrust. We have become a constituency that fears the eventual dissolution of that form of governance we have been taught is our heritage and interminable right. It is fully accepted but too little understood, "The love of liberty is the love of others; the love of power is the love of ourselves," *William Hazlitt, 1820.*

We have an imbalance in our educational system and approach which is seen in the man on the street and elsewhere in struggle for a livelihood, often without having the benefit of the basic skills necessary to survive in today's increasingly complex world. Examination of the curricula of colleges and universities will yield many units as one-sided. Not infrequently they leave the impression that biological traits such as designer garb, endocrine secretions and devotion to the control by the academically privileged are the predominant forces in human development. That ethics and morality and understanding of the need to work toward common goals is in fact at best passé if not outmoded. Education must be tempered and guided by wisdom. Wisdom insists on intellectual honesty and respect for valid facts and a pure motive to seek and preserve the truth. We must institute educational and training systems more available to provide those who only desire a substantive wage from an employment that requires a degree of effort and forethought. We fail to prepare many of our college inhabitants for the reality of the work atmosphere, the broadest and most common denominator if acquiring sufficient income and self-esteem.

Rather, we spew out thousands of individuals with possible fascinating subject matter but useless qualifications allowing the holder to enter the job market on a measurable even level with his fellow graduates. An emphasis on medieval French existentialist literature may be of assistance to someone studying the broad field of literature study itself. It does not fit in the applicant's resume being reviewed by a potential employer looking for someone willing to begin by editing company brochures, newsletters and adding flair to the company's training manuals. The fault is not necessarily the student or potential applicant, it lies within the altruistic and at times narrowly produced curriculums at many colleges and universities. The more exciting, the more unique the title of the course and the mysterious vagaries of the study involved, the quicker the desire to sign up for the course. It remains emotionally galvanizing until that future reader of the resume targets what has been stated as the applicants major in school. It's not a point of discrimination, it's just the real world.

We are a nation proven to be capable to have the constitutional right to govern ourselves. The authority to govern moves when not continually monitored and cautioned, tends to move upward from the constituency. It becomes tantamount of a form of "divine right", the principal argument that upheld kings and rulers for millennia. In America that direct ion must be reversed if ever seen to increase. Here the authority of govern extends upward from the will of the people to those elected to serve as administrators of the people's common good. It must be understood by those in congress that when the federal government demands or attempts to enforces qualification for or compliance with an act in conflict with that state's constitution, it violates the basic principal of state's rights enunciated by our Founding Fathers. That states have the right to maintain their individual sovereignty over local matters and conditions. When challenged it then the courts must enter the fray and determine the interpretation and balance of existing federal and state legal positions.

The law is often seen only as words on paper. Its use is to codify a degree of disciplined societal conduct without imposition of binding restrictions on individual freedom and right of expression of the citizen. The disturbing reality is that the law and its creation, administration and adjudication is performed by humans. We must never forget, we are only given the rights provided us by the society in which we dwell. It is that structure we have to deal with.

With no mandate or granted mandate to prophesy, still I must foretell for my own egoistic benefit, the future as I imagine it can happen given particular situations. If Joe Biden's term is to be successful, it will place him behind the desk in the Oval Office but it will not give him the power of the Chief Executive as determined by Article II of the constitution for a major reason. It will in fact merely place his coterie of political power seekers, rectum bussers and incompetent administration lackeys in place to function openly as the shadow government. Were the policies and promised *progressive* and ultra-liberal changes in economic, social global policies to become legal operating processes and rules of conduct, the following will occur. Industries will once more leave our shores for more favorable tax and labor conditions. Education will fall under the total rule of a government agency. States and local entities will be required to comply with the direction and substance of what and how all permitted subjects shall be taught.

A revised form of what was once referred to as affirmative action will be emplaced. Hiring, promotion, wage and working conditions will be implemented with an automatic inclusion of a minimum number of minorities and a guaranteed minimum supervisory personnel roster of no less than two selected minority groups. Local municipal governments will be cautioned and if non-compliant to the degree desired by the administration, to either fulfill the required national insistence on mandatory diversity, will suffer severe economic penalties. The current disarray of drug laws and related searches and arrests will be totally mollified to the degree that the drug dealer must be first found guilty of much more serious felonies to even be brought to court for any drug related offense. The 2nd Amendment will be seriously threatened to the degree an underground of weapons manufacturing, purchase and ownership will become a criminal act. Other changes still under discussion by the incoming parade of progressive paws will eventually affect every American and created a further divided nation.

Were Donald Trump to have realized realize reelection, the opposition might have immediately moved for another impeachment action and if the Republican Party were to lose its majority in the Senate that method of removal could have become a reality. The media will again support any litany of rumor, supposed revelations and a constant presentation of any and every claim of current and/or past misdeeds. The television channels and news print will be filled with a continuing stream of accusers and contended witnesses to any event or statement imagined or purely fictionalized. Trump, his vice-president and cabinet members would have required added security due to the automatic plethora of physical threats against them and their families by the disappointed leftists. Little will be accomplished in Congress other than attempting to legislate the desired changes continually proposed by the ultra-liberal factions and Biden's new circle of progressive supporters. If followed, shallow and insufficiently sustainable programs will become the sharpening factors for future political and social reverberations and added voter dissatisfaction. A future too blurred by indecision to provide substantive confidence by the the general public.

One cannot totally dismiss the many malefactions of Donald Trump during those years prior to ascending to the White House. Since then he has been portrayed, and not always falsely, as a braggart, self-aggrandizer, excessive in his modern day 'tweeting' on every subject and his tendency to bypass what might be kernels of truth in a number of his pronouncements and assertions. His critics refer to that as lying. However, if we are to assume his many such statements are in fact outright and knowing falsehoods, we then would have to gather as his colloquial colleagues a cadre of the current press corps including the TV news channels and both the New York Times and Washington Post. These conduits of information may someday be revealed as the real culprits in an era of purposeful misrepresentation, prejudice and knowing bias. Somehow we've raced into this age of instant communication so fast that we may have left the recognition of what is actually the truth far behind.

The mendacity of all concerned – for those still struggling with required racial social equality studies at Harvard, Princeton and Columbia - that means untruthfulness – and as sad a fact that might be, it also permeates the entire media, the Halls of Congress. And even those who preach the new, superfluous babble from those gargantuan and grotesque cathedrals of televised religious fraudulency. Biden has said that he was a state school graduate and that he wouldn't be an Ivy Leaguer in the White House. That may be true as far as the difference is concerned by regardless, it is the public reaction to whatever he proposes, promotes or – as critics will contend – is pushed into supporting by forces, not in the Oval Office – just outside and down the hallway.

The universities mentioned are fine, highly reputable institutions of higher learning. They have earned places in the history of the American educational structure. Embarrassingly they have also become havens for a plethora of virulent left wing activists who seem dedicated to creating an increasing cadre of likeminded youths. Young individuals who, through their educational prowess, intelligence and ambition, can and will most likely become the leadership of future political, economic and academic enterprises. Their indoctrination leaves no room for the dissenter, the conservative, the individual who merely desires to question so as to allow a free discussion of potential ramifications of any proposed program or philosophy.

Since developing the basic concept for this work of my individual reflections about the previous five years of viewing the despicable realm of evident and continual hypocrisy known simply as the Washington scene, I've had lasting doubts as to its inclusion. Whether these next comments would be an effect adjunct to my previous thoughts or an aberration of my own dislike for the callous disregard of any ethical standard by the cast members of this modern day draconian drama referred to as politics. Initially we will need to number those on stage right, to use theatrical terms and lessen the individual targeting. Even as Alexandra Ocasio Cortez has introduced herself as the new political force in the party, it would be advisable were she to be more rational and consistently on subject point as she further beleaguers a divided Democratic Party.

The fate of the incumbent in every instance must ultimately be the right of the voters, not the media or even a particular political leadership. The persuasive influence of the seemingly obligatory funding sources cannot be disregarded. The ever rising cost of campaigning will always be the fiscal millstone around the neck of the candidate, whatever office and at whatever level he or she might aspire to. I cannot predict or assume when or if that financial onus will ever be eliminated. To all those younger and newly elected members of Congress who will assume the elevated stature you've worked so hard to attain, remember, our country is not yours to control. Rather, it is yours in which to preserve the best interest, the safeguards and the open vista of opportunity for all citizens, regardless of political, ethnic, religious, economic and social affiliation. To assume any other posture is to violate your oath of office. Winston Churchill summed it our present situation best when he said: "No one pretends that democracy is perfect or all wise. Indeed it has been said that democracy is the worst form of Government, except for all those other forms that have been tried from time to time".

Chapter 15

My Personal Postscript

I feel it necessary to leave the reader with a hopefully brief compilation of my personal position on a number of the heretofore lengthy commentary. First, a private note to President Joseph Biden, rhetorically of course as it will be displayed herein.

"Mr. President, I did not vote for you, nor your opponent as was my refusal to support him in 2016. Although not an advocate of your administration, I wish you success in those areas that are not in conflict with certain aspects of our society and governance many of us have enjoyed for many years. During my lifetime to date I've experience the death in office of one president, the assassination of another, followed by his brother's killing who was at that time a potential candidate for that office. And there was the vicious slaying of Martin Luther King, Jr., the recognized leader of an emerging Civil rights movement, but also a symbol that recognized the need to subject racism to a strong light of inspection. I witnessed the resignation of a president and the impeachment of two other residents of the Oval Office, both fruitless efforts when facing a trial in the Senate.

However, your actions during the first quarter of your administration were rife with excessive pursuit of programs and directions created by executive order and not the mandated consideration by the legislature. That, sir, is hubris of a distasteful nature and unfitting the office of president. During the past 30 years I've watched a dysfunctional legislative posturing and total incapacity for positive considerations on behalf of both the national and individual constituencies of congressional members. Instead, during that same period, I and my fellow citizens have seen the Congress of the United States turn into a group of sniveling, ethical cowards, intent on only enhancing their personal position, stature and incumbency in positions they hold and their efforts to accelerate absorption of greater power. Perhaps a brutal, condemnatory statement, but all too true.

You constantly declare your intent to bring this nation back to some sense of normalcy as you envision its necessary future. However, you must recognize the salient fact; that you are surrounded by a collections of unethical, power hungry political miscreants. If they are your principal advisors, you are faced with a collection of personal agendas, none apparently reflecting the good of the nation and concern for our given constitutional rights. Your vice presidential selection was foisted on you from the distinctly ultra-liberal wing of your party. The person chosen had no the experience, the temperament or the ethical qualifications to fulfill the necessary role of succession were you to be unable to complete your term. Of all the many talented and perceptive women of racially minority status or not, you had this one, not chosen by you, but politically forced upon you.

Surrounded by individuals extremely vocal and vitriolic in their earlier attempts to dethrone your predecessor and their current campaign of promoting extremely costly and as yet fully discussed programs, their innate obsession with total control is undeniable. Unless you can tether their constant intention to overcome any resistance by your office or the opposition party, they will have created the true "deep state" and opposition shadow government your opponent spoke of so frequently over the past five years.

No doubt there was substantive evidence of election count miscues, insufficiencies, errors created by poor training and supervision, untested software, and in a few cases, probable incidental fraud performed by overly ardent supporters of either party. That and the pandemic concerns that forced a quickly formulated and never truly developed voter mail-in system, resulted in a potpourri of confusion, misjudgments and the resultant cries of corrupt election process. As stated earlier, you were legitimately elected. However, those were the controversial and disputed variances in the 2020 election situations. Now, it is your responsibility as the nation's Chief Executive Officer to have an immediate review undertaken and every effort put forward to assure the next election provides a more sound, professionally directed and closely monitored voting process and procedure. This could restore the confidence of those who may not have supported your candidacy that you are in the Oval Office as a direct representative of all the people.

Now, a repeated rebuke of the media, which I've already skewered in a relatively mild manner. To the print and electronic reporters, editors, broadcast anchors and various talk and news shows, get off your mythical white horse of past declarations of non-bias and injection of personal opinion and too often, falsified presentation. Your obvious lack of forthright presentation of the news, depending on the editorial decisions bathed in political allegiance, was one of the primary causes for the increasing public distrust in what was once a supposedly honorable profession. You continue to feel you are the anointed clarions of equality and regardless of proven fact and inviolable truth, you march on, trampling the former image of an honored profession. You debasing the ethics you constantly purport in print and over the airwaves, coupled with the claim of First Amendment rights used as a canopy to hide from the disgust of your criminally assault on of free speech. You continually insult the public you are to serve.

Now we turn our attention to the departed 45th President of the United States, Donald J. Trump. As much as I may have seemed supportive of numerous undertakings of his and some of the early campaign promises, I am fully of the mind that he has left presidential image in veritable disarray. His actions since the election displayed a deplorable lack of conscious recognition that his time was over and that a new movement had garnered the voters' approval. The resulting myriad of litigations and attempted invalidation of the sworn duties of those electoral votes obtained by Biden did nothing but tarnish your image. Your benighted efforts to salvage an already sinking political Titanic, created a carnival atmosphere of those duties each elected official must attend to every two to four years. That said, Mr. Trump, return to your former life, whatever that may be in the face of pending allegations of criminal actions. The White House is no longer your official residence and your future political or business yearnings I leave to the fates as it no longer interests me to any degree.

Mr. President, you are entering the most arduous period of your life. Dire emotional frustration will be very evident. The Speaker of the House, 80-year old matriarch of political mismanagement, strident voices on the extreme left, will continue to both damage your administrative potential and diminish your personally desired legacy. She is permitted too much power tin the desired free flow of discussion, review and either passage or failure of legislation. She is the dam that holds back that expected a flow of measures legislated in only the country's best interest and not her and her ideological colleagues. It is hoped your Vice President she will not be seen daily reading the obituaries in the Washington Post to determine which office will be hers that day.

Gathered into this coterie of individuals, callous in their disdain for the average citizen is, at the time of this writing, the majority leader of the Senate, whose leadership to date an ideological disaster. Across the way in the House sits Representatives whose partisan venality and inappropriate comments have disgraced the elected positions they hold. Alexandra Ocasio Cortez at this time is the youngest of that group, and whose strident voice has become irritating to even the most progressive advocates. Hopefully she is not the symbol of a rising generation in the Democratic Party. When speaking of issues so important to our nation, she has inadvertently copied one of Donald Trump's most evident flaws, opening her mouth before engaging her brain. They and your cabinet selections are critical as they form the credo of your administrative format. However, you have a number of new appointees already reflecting a degree of inconsequential purpose. They are among the weak links in the chain of resolute action that is so needed during these chaotic times.

Your Federal Bureau of Investigation (FBI) is headed by and still invested in conspicuously anti-Trump devotees that form its hierarchy. Their past transgressions in earlier investigations of Trump, not yet fully revealed. But that is the situation you will face Mr. President. Never knowing if their prior bias and politically based enmity might impinge on a fair application of the Rule of Law that may become at issue with your predecessors future legal difficulties. Or any other such legal entanglements that might face your associates. It must be warned, regardless of their earlier target, this totally inappropriate and criminally liable continuance of distorting heir oath and and obligation to the long held image of the Bureau can only bear fruit of later ethical disregard.

Hopefully Mr. President, having spent almost five decades dwelling in that brackish backwater of deceit called Washington politics, you should recognize what your predecessor aptly called, "the swamp." There was bias and advertent misdeed in a number of DOJ actions and among that of certain FBI hierarchy. There actions, whether individual or as an agency approved policy allowed both surreptitious and obvious prejudice and legal chicanery. It must be expunged before the disease of personal devotion to particular political affiliations totally overrides the absolute need for impartiality in every investigative undertaking. There are still possibly signs of the mold of personal agendas remaining in those related law enforcement agencies.

But more closely to the core of your future vexations is the looming approach of whatever may be fully revealed about your family's involvement in activities either suspicious in nature or already under investigation. As to still unproven charges of your possible knowledge of and involvement in such questionable undertakings based on your influence a few years ago, these need clarification and where viable, rebuttal. This entire predicament must be dealt with, openly and let the proverbial chips lie where they fall. Not being totally knowledgeable of the particular aspects of any charges or accusations, I only hope the bias I spoke of earlier will not inhibit proper and sufficient investigation and eventually resolution.

The right to protest is considered a sacred rule of constitutional protection of the individual citizen. Contrary to the absolutism of this possession by some, there must be legal and demonstrative controls when this right becomes the vehicle for violence, destruction, intimidation, threat, injury or death to collateral victims. The Black Lives Matters actions may be felt by some less rational individuals as fully authorized and permitted under that particular phrase in the First Amendment. That is the unperceptive view of those who contend this particular constitutional allowance is an unlimited access to anarchy. Regardless of the original purposes expressed by the ensuing protest organizers, what happened to ignite these fires of supposed retribution has been addressed and will be the hallmark of desired future changes and reformation of past law enforcement transgressions. The inability or lack of desire by the Black Lives Matters movement to control and eliminate to reoccurring community devastation was coupled with the cowardice of numerous local municipal authorities and legislative bodies to take immediate and meaningful action displayed wanton political cowardice.

The past misdeeds of certain police officers and the apparent lack of real concern and attention to community minority and racial sensitivities, must be addressed very soon. Yet, with the injudicious nature of too many local administrations, coupled with the increasing pressure of the debilitating pandemic effect, this reformation or reworking of our law enforcement approach to minorities, may still be a distance afar. The questions remain. Who actually directs the activities of the BLM? From whom and where comes the funding necessary to support their organizational efforts? Until such information is forthcoming, they will remain an illusionary composite of both good and evil.

During this essay, the writer has been less than charitable to the membership of our national Congress. However, there exists this continuing lethargy to perform legislative requirements, to consider and move either way on proposed legislation and to address current issues with definitive and substantive hearings, intended to lead to possible legal resolution. These periods of inactivity have been incipient since the early days of our founding. More often than not, ceasing when major national disaster or the threat of war appeared on the horizon. Without such crisis's, could it just be the boredom of constant, inconsequential speeches by fellow legislators, the brief work weeks or the desire to spend more time with family and supporters in one's home district – or the oppressive summer heat or brutal winters that encompass our nation's capital on occasion?

Yet, we still keep electing those same individuals who keep ignoring or avoiding their oaths to maintain the sole consideration of their constituency.

There are four areas of imposed although suspect immunity responsibility when it comes to speech between two individuals. The prohibition that prohibits the priest from reporting even the most venal act or hideous, revelation by in individual seeking the sanctuary of the confessional or in private conversation as a supplicant. Second, the supposed inviolate rule of attorney/client relationship. Third, the traditional doctor/patient association even extending to those who carry such title into near non-related medical fields. Fourth, and possibly the most abused and too often misused right, the so-called journalist freedom from ever revealing the anonymous source to a stated accusation, claim of felonious action by an unnamed perpetrator. Too often the truth or reliable facts of a reported incident or situation is hidden by the stench of a landfill of anonymous sources.

As for the religious representative, I refuse to delve into that abyss of incongruous morality and doctrinal allowed evasion. The years of protecting anything said between an attorney and his or her client is one only the legislative powers can adjust if needed. There are, however, certain waivers in perpetuating that particular privilege. The medical prohibition of disclosing private and personal medical information to all but authorized individuals such as immediate family, legal guardians and unless permitted by the patients themselves, creates a sensitive conundrum. One geared to protect an important issue of privacy. In reviewing the increasing and irresponsible dispensation of rumors, hearsay, unfounded allegations and reiteration of that which has never been proven, the media has exceeded its declared journalistic rights. Use of the term anonymous or high ranking, but unidentified source is a tool to add legitimacy to an article or a reported comment. It becomes becomes semantic legerdemain, easily disguising the absence of fact or overt bias on the part of the reporter or commentator.

To the novice acolyte at the altar of the political cathedral, more simply termed, the nation's capital, the first hesitant access must be intimidating. To be at the seat of the government, the realm of the elected presidential sultanate, the place where influence and intrigue mix to form the stench of empowerment. The simple description of a president's job is to get as many people as he can to do many things for him – or her. And for these individuals to feel each task, each assignment is a sign of their acceptance into the coveted gathering of the special people. If and when any assignment were to run afoul of investigation by the opposition, bringing the shadow of blame, it will be the individual assigned the task who will suffer the consequences. Or in good political parlance, literally fall on their swords. It is the price one pays to enter the world in which they may be ill prepared to survive.

In order to once more require the free flow of information and the desire of representatives for their proposed bills to ever see the light of reasonable discussion and compromise where needed, a major change is required. The positions and rules of conduct for speaker of the House of Representatives and the Majority Leaders of either party must be revised. Their dictatorial control, their apparent demand for unencumbered demand for power is not reasonably evidenced by constitutional formation and has brought this country to its political and economic knees. In addition, term limits for all members of congress must be emplaced. Age and years within the control function does not automatically may assure added wisdom or ability to direct the country's welfare to the most equitable level. However, it can create the rancidity of self-aggrandizement and fiscal gain. It speaks to a totalitarian tenure, an overwhelming sense of privilege and absolutism of opinion. That violates the true intent of freedom of expression by those elected to speak the needs of the voters they represent.

As for those comments relative to the various brands of religious teachings and assurances of salvation – by whatever means or both personal financial, or emotional cost, the truth remains. It is the caulking of human resolution and belief that keeps the bricks all the houses of worship standing. Still manifest is the need of those religions professing the total emphasis on the human spirit's trip to what form of haven is doctrinally taught and correct those past and present evils that demean their intent. Religion is the beating heart of the more traditionally oriented and conservative individual. It must become a reflection of personal interest and not a tool of group divisiveness. Its leadership, whatever the form, should not be allowed to destroy the free will of the believer. Additionally, its entry into the political marketplace must be thoroughly vetted before becoming a contended right not referred to in the constitution.

For my comments on the various principle religious groups or sects, I would offer just the following caveats. To the Roman Catholic Church, rid yourself of the *bad apples* in your barrel of clergy. Don't just distance yourself from their iniquities and either ignore their crimes or send them off to meditation in some undisclosed location, sans any punishment. His must be the concern of the doctrinal teachings of the church, faithfulness to God's commandments and rules as the church determines and requires. He is not to become a pseudo member of the United Nations or the outspoken clarion of certain subject that remain in the domain of individual cultures or societies or nations.

To Islam, distance yourself, both organizationally and theologically from those who would slaughter innocents, demand elimination of certain ethnic entities. And do it in a fashion that refers directly to Allah's desire to be sincere in its declarations of innocence and desire to be one with the world. The Islamic culture, is notable for its advances in art and architecture, its unique contributions to the world of mathematics and engineering innovation. To have this unrivaled history of accomplishment sullied by the irrational acts of the ignorant and rebellious rabble is a stain on the sayings of its founder, Mohammed.

To the Church of Jesus Christ of Latter Day Saints, rid your past history of the more imperceptible elements of the original years ago in the now well known "Book of Mormon," creating certain situations and locations still unfounded. You have a strong base of theological substance, you family ideals are copied by numerous other religions. Your history, although an interesting read, is still filled with inaccuracies and contended incidents that when disclosed as the results of a fertile mind, cast aspersions on your faith. You have an intended objective of fairness in dealing with other faiths and social proclivities, however critical they may be to your doctrine or the insult and intolerance you've suffered over the past one hundred and ninety years. Your message is more often resounded in the unparalleled music and voices of the internationally renowned and magnificent Mormon Tabernacle Choir.

The Jewish faith, its history and legends, its teachings and notable figures predates all the other theologies mention by thousands of years. Early developers of parts of the barren deserts and mountains of the middle east, they have overcome deprivation, enslavement, conflict and the horrible attempt of both the Nazi regime of Adolf Hitler and tyranny of Josef Stalin to annihilate them as a people and a culture. Considered by some as rigid in their teachings and rules of conduct, nevertheless they became substantive factors in the economy and social life of many countries, only to continually face the ever present barrier of anti-Semitism. This is a cancerous malady that still today, fosters criminal and social actions against them throughout the world and is unacceptably still rampant in our country. Mr. President, it resides as firmly in our nation as anywhere else in the world. Be attentive to its rise and move to take appropriate action to eliminate its influence and effect on your total constituency.

To the evangelically driven soothsayers, pseudo prophets and diviners of dogmas that seem at times to have little reference to fact or reality, dismantle your tents of old, your more recent cavernous TV studios and your constant claim to a divine understanding and connection that never did nor ever will exist. Like the carnival barker of old and the snake oil salesman of our earlier, more rural days, to use one of our younger societies more modern expressions, *get a life,* or better yet, get a real job. And to the denominational cults and simulated religiosity, you're merely picking the pockets of the unwary or uniformed which needs to stop.

This is not a declaration of atheism or agnosticism. I merely hope to clarify the disparities that still fascinatingly combine to form what is considered a religious condition but is more an amalgamation of individualism and much varied beliefs. Held by a people who have the right to decide their particular future – post life. It is not my intent to demean the devout reader of scriptures and the works of different doctrinal or theological writers. For centuries, Jews have been chastised for the death of the purported messiah, Jesus Christ. This became an erroneous linkage condemning the Jewish people to centuries of abuse, suffering and discrimination for the past two thousand years. Regrettably it still forms the basic precept that alienated most Christian sects from the faith of Abraham.

The year 2020 was one of increased threat by a devastating pandemic and the rise in global tensions between numerous governments and ideologies. The economy, whatever its form, remains a major concern of most American citizens and even more so by the increasing numbers of undocumented individuals who desire better than what they fled their native land to achieve. You need to issue to national, state and local legislatures, a simple axiom. Either lead or get out of the way. To the immoderate, liberal enthusiast, history must be rewritten, unfortunately by those with little or no intuitive or substantive knowledge of when and how such previous reports were ever developed, and often by whom. If we destroy our archival past with versions the new scribes may have little understanding of, we will eliminate remembrance of that which happened from which we learn, educate our children and can, at times, find pride and appreciation if the achievement of the participants.

Finally, to the new world advocates, the global oneness concept and the equality obsessed, regardless of what it truly means. The deaths of a number of black people, sometimes because of unauthorized or illegal action by certain law enforcement officers, was grounds for outrage and demand for reformation. It did not however countenance or ennoble the concerted actions of a group whose violence and destruction served no valid purpose. No civilized entity can exist in a continuing demand for recognition at the end of a gun barrel or flaming torch or assault upon those assigned to protect the overall security of any and all in attendance. The increasing influence of the national political figure, the celebrity and the media cannot be allowed to continually put their thumbs on the scales of justice. You Mr. Biden, are the elected guardian of our freedoms, custodian of our constitutional rights and the spokesperson to world for every American citizen. That is is the responsibility and burden you accepted when you swore the oath of the presidency.

At the start of this book, the then residing president was accused of seditious, creating or advocating insurrection through a mob attack on the capitol building during the Electoral Vote count by the Congress. There was actual entry into portions of the building by members of the riotous group and damage occurred and regrettably the loss of a few lives. The ensuing media frenzy and hysterical condemnations and movement for immediate removal of Donald Trump became the daily news of the day. Demands ensued for his impeachment or implementation of the 25th Amendment which permits a sitting president's immediate removal and became the call by members of both parties. As to the results of either proposed method I leave that to other writers and experts in those fields.

As a result of the horrific sight of individuals attempting to actually seize control of our governmental center in a violent and totally inexcusable fashion eventually a theoretical resolution occurred. The previous president, now a private citizen, was vilified incessantly by a media and parts of the reigning political power. After failed impeachment attempt a second time, undoubtedly he will be the target of a volley of legal assaults on his past activities and financial holdings. Thus I must leave any future prognostication to those who dwell in that dubious world of conjecture. With the mid-session elections a mere less than two years in the distance, the Democratic Party surely needs to remember the saying, "when seeking to slay the other for revenge, first dig two graves." Although I was not one of the seventy four million who voted for Donald Trump, all those House of Representatives and one third of the Senate preparing for the next election, could soon feel the chill of rebuke by disgruntled and disenchanted voters.

When one group determines to express their cause more violent action and destruction and injury or death is imposed on the non-involved public, there will be retaliation. Plainly stated, there could be blood on the streets. Our younger generation has notified us they are moving toward a new societal configuration where equality is required in all forms. The caveat to all protest groups, as long as the movement's intent is clearly enunciated and violence refused, the right continues. But beware of the tendency to stumble during accelerated fervor. Equilibrium is necessary to assure responsible civic reason and common sense.

*

Mr. President, now that you are in charge, now you are the leader of the most powerful nation in the world, remember, "Pertransvit gladius," `the sword is passed.' Thus, I herewith respectfully submit; "Tomorrow lies in wait within the shadow of your future. Yesterday resides in the deepening twilight of your memory, yet, the clearest view one can have is what is happening today."

About the author

James Oshust has, during a fifty year career, managed major entertainment, sports and exhibition facilities, served in management roles in two Olympic Games, consulted on two others and been part of the management team for the 1994 World Cup Soccer Championship and 1998 Goodwill Games in New York City. He has been an executive with one of the original professional soccer teams in the US and a member of consulting teams for over forty facility design and operations projects domestically, and abroad. He is the author of five books including a personal review of his unique opinions and a citizen's review of the US Constitution. He and his wife, Barbara Walsh Oshust, a former professional ice skater and recognized artist, reside in Millcreek, UT, adjacent to Salt Lake City.